Life Basic Training

A Biblical Examination of Value Systems

Ralph W. Neighbour Jr.

TOUCH Outreach Ministries
Houston, TX 77079

ISBN Number 1-880828-57-X

Printed in the United States of America

1

ARE WE
SIGNIFICANT?

PERSONAL INVENTORY

Just before watching the videotape, thoughtfully answer these questions...

	AGREE	UNCERTAIN	DISAGREE
When someone compliments me, I feel better about myself.	☐	☐	☐
When I really "blow it," I feel very insignificant.	☐	☐	☐
When I do something well, others see me as a more significant person.	☐	☐	☐
Working in church activities causes me to feel significant.	☐	☐	☐
My pastor sees me as more significant when I take a leadership job.	☐	☐	☐
If I could control time more efficiently, I would be a more significant person.	☐	☐	☐
When I fail, I still feel significant.	☐	☐	☐
I become more significant to God when I am actively involved in His work.	☐	☐	☐
If I do not have the funds to live as well as my friends, I feel insignificant.	☐	☐	☐
Unless I live a good life, I am not significant in God's eyes.	☐	☐	☐

VIDEO PRESENTATION

Divide the Outline among the group members to review after video is viewed.

ARE WE SIGNIFICANT?

1. **WHAT IS LIFE ALL ABOUT?**
   A. Most people never think about its meaning
      1. For some, life is too miserable to think about its meaning
      2. For others, life is too much fun to worry about
      3. By not focusing on it, we become "hollow people"
   B. Earthly life is temporary; foolish to live thoughtlessly!

2. **LIFE AS ADAM'S CHILDREN LIVE IT**
   A. What we inherit from Adam:
      1. Physical life
      2. Loss of relationship with God
   B. How Adam's children become "significant"
      1. By their performance
      2. By what we and others think of it
   C. Even church activities can be used in this way

3. **LIFE AS GOD'S CHILDREN LIVE IT**
   A. The significance of the cross
      1. The payment for our adoption
      2. The proof of God's great love
      3. The entrance into a permanent relationship with God
   B. The requirements for Sonship
      1. A desire to have a relationship with God
      2. A readiness to be adopted

4. **THE RIGHTS OF THE ADOPTED CHILD**
   A. Parent cannot ever disown the child
   B. Parent gives his name to child
   C. Parent provides home, lifestyle, love for child
   D. Parent provides protection at all times
   E. Parent includes child in his will

5. **WHAT MAKES CHRISTIANS SIGNIFICANT**
   A. Our adoption...nothing else!
   B. Our relationship makes us significant
      1. No tasks required, no obligations to fulfill
      2. The significance of the cross leaves nothing for us to do

6. **OUR SIGNIFICANCE COMES FROM WHO WE ARE, NOT FROM WHAT WE DO!**

DISCUSSION TOPICS

Always begin with your DAILY REPORT TIME
Let each person share briefly;
report insights gained by completing
the Practical Assignment.

IF YOU HAVE NOT ARRANGED YOURSELVES INTO GROUPS OF FIVE, DO SO AT THIS TIME. GROUPS USUALLY STAY TOGETHER FOR THE ENTIRE COURSE

READ ALOUD LUKE 10:38-42

DISCUSSION QUESTIONS: 30 MINUTES
(NOTE: Divide your time equally among the three
questions. Ask one of the group to be timekeeper.)

1. As a Group, who do we identify with most easily...Mary, or Martha? Why? What are each of them doing to be "significant?"

2. Norm Wakefield says, "A *value* is something that is actually *important enough to be expressed in my daily choices.*" What values, therefore, are being expressed by Mary and Martha?

3. Think now of your own daily choices. Share what you consider to be the most important thing you do on a daily basis. What values are expressed by this? *Do you gain your "significance" from this important thing?*

This is your PRACTICAL ASSIGNMENT for this coming week...

FROM YOUR CONTACTS, SELECT THREE PERSONS WITH WHOM YOU'LL SPEND TIME THIS WEEK. WHAT DO THEY DO TO FEEL SIGNIFICANT? WHAT PERSONS MAKE THEM FEEL SIGNIFICANT? (YOU NEED NOT DISCUSS YOUR OBSERVATIONS WITH THEM.)

WHAT IS THE PURPOSE OF THESE PRACTICAL ASSIGNMENTS?

Your motive for taking this course is to GROW as a Christian! Several ingredients must be mixed together for that growth to take place:

...A STATEMENT OF CHRISTIAN VALUES MUST BE HEARD.
The **videotapes** are prepared to make that statement to you. Each segment will build on the Biblical principles for living life. The quiz you take just before watching it will help you set your mind to hear the material. By itself, this will not be enough to reach the objective!

...A SHAPING OF CHRISTIAN VALUES MUST FOLLOW.
The **small group activities** will let you interact with your friends as you discuss Christian values for living. They will make an impact...but group times alone will not be enough. The next steps must also be taken.

...THE SETTING OF THESE PRINCIPLES IN YOUR MIND MUST BE ADDED.
That's the purpose for spending ten minutes for five days each week in the **DAILY GROWTH GUIDE.** This review of truths you are gathering will cause them to remain in your value system.

...LIVING OUT THESE VALUES IS THE FINAL INGREDIENT.
The **weekly assignment** will take theory and apply it! Each one is designed to fit your normal lifestyle. None are so demanding that you cannot do them. Most permit you to simply observe. As you return to your group for each new session, you will share your observations, thus enriching others. Listen intently to the group's findings. You may discover striking similarities in your findings. Insights gained will help shape your own values.

SUGGESTIONS FOR COMPLETING YOUR ASSIGNMENT...

What do these persons do when they fail to *feel* significant?

Who are the *persons* they desire to impress, to see them as significant?

From *what source* do they gain their significance?

PRACTICAL ASSIGNMENT

FROM YOUR OBSERVATIONS, LIST BELOW THE THINGS PEOPLE YOU HAVE OBSERVED ARE DOING TO FEEL SIGNIFICANT:

ON WHAT BASIS DO THEY SEEK TO BUILD RELATIONSHIPS?

Name _____

DAILY GROWTH GUIDE

OUR
REAL
SIGNIFICANCE

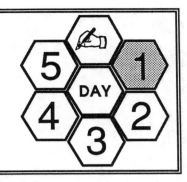

DAY ONE: WHAT MADE MARTHA FEEL SIGNIFICANT?
SCRIPTURE READING: LUKE 10:38-42

1. Which sister would probably make the following statements?

Martha   Mary

☐   ☐   "My performance is the most important thing in my life."

☐   ☐   "Being is far more important than doing."

☐   ☐   "Our performance is important, but secondary."

☐   ☐   "Impressing others is important. Put your best foot forward."

☐   ☐   "When I have not done well I have a feeling of worthlessness."

☐   ☐   "My significance is based on my relationship with God."

☐   ☐   "I worry about what others think of me."

☐   ☐   "Persons are the rare jewels in God's universe."

2. Check the items below which make you feel significant:

☐ Possessions (car, house, clothes, bank account)

☐ Regular, meaningful times of fellowship with the Father through prayer

☐ My friends, who compliment me on my achievements

☐ The knowledge that I am deeply loved by God

☐ My performance at work or in the classroom

☐ Sharing the news of my adoption with Adam's children

☐ My talents and abilities (athletic, music, business, etc.)

ON THE BASIS OF YOUR ANSWERS, ARE YOU MORE LIKE MARY OR MARTHA?

THOUGHT FOR THE DAY:
MY GREATEST NEED IN LIFE IS TO FEEL SIGNIFICANT. ALL MY
PERSONAL PROBLEMS, APART FROM PHYSICAL ILLNESS, STEM FROM
TRYING TO MEET THIS NEED. WHENEVER I BASE MY WORTH UPON MY
PERFORMANCE, I MAKE A SERIOUS MISTAKE. MY TRUE SIGNIFICANCE
IS ROOTED ONLY IN MY RELATIONSHIP WITH THE FATHER.

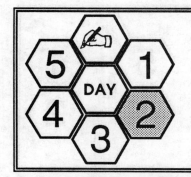

DAILY GROWTH GUIDE

OUR REAL SIGNIFICANCE

DAY TWO: WHAT MADE MARY FEEL SIGNIFICANT?

SCRIPTURE READING: LUKE 10:39

1. **How did Mary relate to Jesus when He came to Bethany?**
   (Check answer)
   - [ ] By honoring Him with an elaborate meal
   - [ ] By hearing His instructions
   - [ ] By allowing Martha's opinions to determine her conduct

2. **What did Jesus consider most important?**
   - [ ] Hard work and lavish hospitality
   - [ ] A total inactive lifestyle
   - [ ] Listening to His word

3. **In your opinion, how did Mary view Martha's busy life?**

4. **If you had been Mary, would Martha's resentment affect you? How?**

5. **In Mary's value system, what made her feel significant?**
   - [ ] Pleasing those who set performance requirements for her
   - [ ] Escaping tasks which did not make her feel significant
   - [ ] Relating with Christ, enjoying the chance to fellowship with Him

6. **In your opinion, which sister had the most significant lifestyle?**
   - [ ] Mary [ ] Martha   Why?_____

   _____

THOUGHT FOR THE DAY:
MY ACTIONS ARE ALWAYS THE RESULT OF MY CONVICTIONS. THEY ARE NEVER HYPOCRITICAL, NEVER CONTRADICTORY. IF MY ACTIONS ARE NOT IN KEEPING WITH JESUS' TEACHINGS, IT IS BECAUSE I DO NOT ACCEPT THEM...NO MATTER HOW LOUDLY I MAY CLAIM OTHERWISE!

DAILY GROWTH GUIDE

OUR
REAL
SIGNIFICANCE

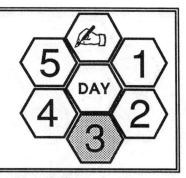

DAY THREE: HOW DID JESUS EVALUATE MARTHA'S LIFESTYLE?
SCRIPTURE READING: LUKE 10:42

1. After reading the following, rewrite it in your own words:

"Now Martha was distracted by her many tasks, so she came to Him and said, 'Lord, do you not care that my sister has left me to get on with the work by myself? Tell her to come and lend a hand.'"

2. As you rewrote her words, what emotions did you sense inside Martha?

☐ Jealousy   ☐ Anger   ☐ Frustration   ☐ Self-Confidence

☐ Inner Peace   ☐ Joy   ☐ Love   ☐ Long Term Conflict

☐ Deep Insecurity   ☐ Need to be Recognized as Significant

3. Jesus told Martha, "One thing is necessary." What did He mean?

☐ One dish of food would have been sufficient

☐ A simple lifestyle is preferable to being a workaholic

☐ Servants must listen to the Master before they can do His work

4. Compare your lifestyle with Martha's. How does Jesus evaluate hers...and yours?

(Jot down your reflections in the space below...)

THOUGHT FOR THE DAY:
IT TAKES RAW WILL POWER TO BEHAVE IN A MANNER THAT VIOLATES
MY TRUE BELIEFS. I CAN PLAY-ACT FOR ONLY SO LONG...AND THEN I
RETURN AGAIN TO MY TRUE BEHAVIOR. I CANNOT RUN AWAY FROM
WHO I TRULY AM.

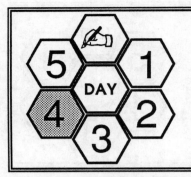

DAILY GROWTH GUIDE

OUR
REAL
SIGNIFICANCE

DAY FOUR: WHAT LIFESTYLE DOES JESUS RECOMMEND?
SCRIPTURE READING: MATTHEW 6:25-33

According to Jesus' teaching here, which statements below are true?
(Place an "X" by the ones you feel match His teaching)

- [ ] I am more significant to God than anything else He has created.
- [ ] I am alone. The universe is my enemy. I must survive!
- [ ] If I do not look out for my own needs, no one else will.
- [ ] Worrying about my future needs is an act of atheism.
- [ ] My worth centers in my relationship with God, not in possessions or people.
- [ ] I will focus my heart on God's ownership of me, and trust Him for tomorrow.
- [ ] Hoarding my personal wealth is a flat rejection of God's promises.
- [ ] Gaining my significance from my accomplishments is an act of faith.
- [ ] The Master can be trusted to care for His servant's needs.
- [ ] Worry and anxiety waste energy, but achieve nothing at all.
- [ ] The most important resource in the world is locked up in my own mind.
- [ ] God wants us to be lazy, sitting around uselessly, being "spiritual".
- [ ] Being consumed with meeting my own needs is a dead-end street.
- [ ] My talents, my gifts, are God's treasury, from which I can give to others.
- [ ] Life is to be enjoyed. God is going to meet needs as they arise.
- [ ] Martha's lifestyle was a contradiction of these verses.
- [ ] Mary had chosen the best of all: fellowship with her Lord.

THOUGHT FOR THE DAY:
I ALWAYS LIVE BY FAITH! MY ACTIONS REVEAL IN WHAT, OR IN WHOM, I HAVE PLACED MY FAITH. EVERY CHOICE IS MADE BECAUSE I BELIEVE CERTAIN THINGS TO BE TRUE. UNFORTUNATELY, MOST OF MY BELIEFS WERE GATHERED THOUGHTLESSLY, LIKE I GATHER GERMS...AWARE I CONTAIN THEM, BUT NO IDEA WHERE THEY CAME FROM.

DAILY GROWTH GUIDE

OUR
REAL
SIGNIFICANCE

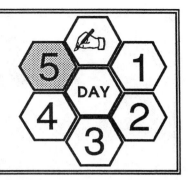

DAY FIVE: WHAT MAKES ME SIGNIFICANT?
SCRIPTURE READING 1 JOHN 3:1-3

A mother holds her newborn infant in her arms. That child is significant to her! You may ask, "Why? The child has not accomplished a thing. It cannot earn money, and it cannot help her. Why should it be significant?" You know the answer: that child's significance to the mother is simply the fact that *the child exists.*

So it is with you...your greatest value is simply that you are God's child. That's what John meant in this verse: **"How great is the love that the Father has shown to us! We were called God's children, and such we are..."** Apart from any performance on your part, He loves you simply because you are His child.

Once you have accepted that truth, you will understand that no activity in life is as important as fellowshipping with Him. And, no achievement in life is so important that it can displace fellowship with Him.

But something else will come into focus. You are released from the emotional storms that rage within those who feel their only significance is in what they do, in what they earn, in what they control, or in honors they have achieved.

Once you realize your significance comes strictly from your relationship with the Father, you are free to be productive and useful, using your talents and your gifts in ways that are meaningful to yourself and to others. You need never again feel the pressure to become important because of what you have accomplished.

Prepare to swim against the stream of your culture as you live by this truth! All the Children of Adam, without exception, gain their significance by their status, by their distinctions. One is a great bowler; another, known for an ability to decorate; others for intellect, wealth, business sense, scholarship, musical ability, etc. They will evaluate you by their standards. Even as Mary faced the harsh criticism of Martha, so you will be misunderstood.

You are forever significant, simply because you are the child of God! Excel in any task...be effective in any area you choose...and enjoy every minute of it! You are forever free of the stress of having to climb some tall mountain to prove you have worth, that you can be "on top." Leave those foolish tasks to Adam's children. They have nothing *better* to do with their lives!

> *THOUGHT FOR THE DAY:*
> *WHAT I BELIEVE IS WHAT I DO. BELIEFS TAKE TIME TO BECOME ROOTED. FALSE BELIEFS WITH DEEP ROOTS ARE REMOVED ONLY WITH EMBATTLED DETERMINATION. NEW BELIEFS MUST BE DELIBERATELY SELECTED OVER AND OVER AGAIN. FINALLY, THEY WILL BECOME DEEPLY ROOTED, AND I WILL RESPOND AUTOMATICALLY TO THEM.*

Thought For The Week

I WAS HUNGRY

I was hungry and you formed a humanities club and discussed my hunger. Thank you

I was imprisoned and you crept off quietly to your chapel and prayed for my release. Thank you.

I was naked and in your mind you debated the morality of my appearance. Thank you.

I was homeless and you preached to me of the spiritual shelter of the love of God. Thank you.

I was lonely and you left me alone to pray for me. Thank you.

You seem so holy, so close to God. But I'm still very hungry and lonely and cold.

Source Unknown

"For I was hungry, and you gave me no food; I was thirsty, and you gave me no drink; I was a stranger and you did not take me in; ...Inasmuch as you have not done it to the least of my brethren, you have not done it unto me."

● *Matthew 25:42-45*

2

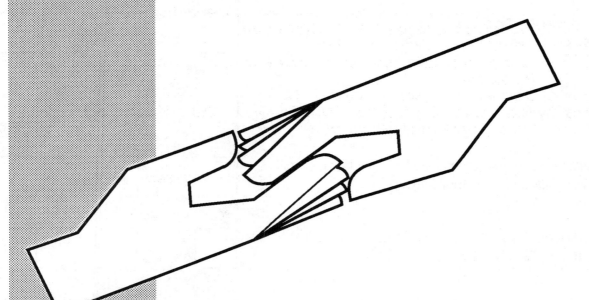

IS WHAT WE DO
SIGNIFICANT?

PERSONAL INVENTORY

Just before watching the videotape, thoughtfully answer these questions...

	AGREE	UNCERTAIN	DISAGREE
My actions are not important, since I am significant to God regardless of what I do.	☐	☐	☐
I serve God because this is what I ought to do as a Christian.	☐	☐	☐
I pray because God commanded it in scripture, and I feel an obligation to do so.	☐	☐	☐
If I do wrong, God will allow some calamity to come into my life.	☐	☐	☐
While I know salvation is by faith, God expects me to live a good Christian life.	☐	☐	☐
The most important thing as a Christian is to try to find what God's will is for me.	☐	☐	☐
Witnessing is something I do when we have visitation or special "pushes" for new converts.	☐	☐	☐
Sharing Christ with others is absolutely the most important thing I ever do.	☐	☐	☐
I am so involved in church activities I have no time to be with non-Christians.	☐	☐	☐
If I introduce many to Jesus Christ, God sees me as a more significant person.	☐	☐	☐

VIDEO PRESENTATION

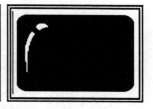

Divide the Outline among the group members to review after video is viewed.

IS WHAT WE DO SIGNIFICANT?

1. **OUR NEW LIFE STYLE**
   A Begins with faith in the Father
      1. God keeps His promises
      2. Until we take the step of faith, we have none
      3. Once taken, we have all the faith there is
   B. Now we are significant...because we're adopted

2. **ENTERING OUR NEW LIFE STYLE**
   A "Kingdom" - place where God reigns as Master
      1. Our King asks us to become "Administrators"
      2. This is a deliberate choice on our part
   B. Two lifestyles among God's children
      1. Enjoy benefits, become significant "Adam's way"
      2. Accept our significance, become an Administrator
   C. Choice of lifestyles changes way we function

3. **AN ALLEGORY ILLUSTRATING TWO LIFESTYLES**
   A Contrast of two brothers in the "family"
      1. James: close relationship with the Father
      2. Alfred: determined to be "Number one"
      3. Same house, radically different lifestyles
   B. Their attitudes toward the Father
      1. Both love and respect him
      2. Only James desires to spend time with him

4. **THE FATHER'S PROPOSAL**
   A His deep love for the Children of Adam
   B. His willingness to share his wealth with his sons
   C. Requests they become Administrators
   D. Objective: encourage Sons of Adam to be adopted
   E. Balance of their lifestyles left free

5. **THE SON'S REACTION**
   A James: no real love for Adam's children
   B. Alfred: no desire to do the Father's will
      1. He enjoys the provisions of his adopted life
      2. He thinks and lives like a Son of Adam

6. **SUMMARY**
   A Our relationship with God isn't related to works
   B. We now qualify to be His Administrators
   C. Doing so doesn't increase our worth - but it reflects our love!

DISCUSSION TOPICS

Always begin with your DAILY REPORT TIME
Let each person share briefly;
report insights gained by completing
the Practical Assignment.

DAILY REPORT TIME: (10 minutes) Let each person share for no more than 1 minute, reporting insights gained from the weekly assignment. Then use the remaining portion of the 10 minutes for a general discussion of your findings.

A WORD TO THE WISE...nothing is more frustrating in a group life than a participant who overtalks! Be sensitive to the time limits set for sharing. In Daily Report Times, you will always have only one minute per person for your report, followed by five minutes for group sharing. Thanks!

DISCUSSION QUESTIONS: 20 Minutes
(Note: As you did last week, divide your time equally among the questions. Pass the timekeeper task to a new person in the group each week.)

1. Look into the future: what problems do you forecast for this Father and his two sons, James and Alfred?

2. Which son do you feel most closely represents your own inner struggles? Let each person answer. Then discuss the reasons for your choices.

3. How will the Father react when he learns that neither one of his sons will agree to his offer? Why? How would *you* react if you were the Father? Why?

This is your PRACTICAL ASSIGNMENT for this coming week...

FROM YOUR OIKOS LIST, SELECT ONE CHRISTIAN WHO IS SIMILAR TO JAMES AND ONE WHO IS SIMILAR TO ALFRED. YOU HAVE A CHOICE: SIMPLY OBSERVE THEM, OR DISCUSS THE QUESTIONS BELOW WITH THEM.

In the Allegory, James had difficulty loving the children of Adam. **What are the characteristics of those who love God, but have no concern for those who do not know Christ?**

Alfred had difficulty reorganizing his life around his Father's value system. **What are the conflicts within those who live by their own values, rejecting those of the Father?**

You may answer these questions by OBSERVATION, DISCUSSION WITH FRIENDS, or a COMBINATION OF BOTH.

...QUESTIONS REGARDING "JAMES" TYPES OF CHRISTIANS:

How do they reconcile God's compassion for the world with their own preoccupation with personal Bible study and "spiritual growth?" How do they feel about having been active Christians for years without ever sharing their faith?

How do they rationalize their desire to fellowship with the Father, yet not honor His request that they tell the Sons of Adam He wants to adopt them?

"James" types are often found among the "pillars" of the church. How are they able to display their public churchgoing without displaying concern for those who never darken the doors of a church building? (Remember, their conduct is quite rational in their own eyes!)

...QUESTIONS REGARDING THE "ALFRED" TYPES OF CHRISTIANS:

How much value do they place on prayer and Bible study, as compared to the value placed on socializing, possessions, or recreational activities?

How much understanding of God do they have? Is He truly known by them? Have they ever desired a deep, personal connection with Him?

From what source **do** they gain satisfaction? Something or someone must be meeting "felt needs" in their lives...or they would be dissatisfied with their lifestyle. To understand these sources of satisfaction is to understand them!

PRACTICAL ASSIGNMENT

LIST BELOW YOUR INSIGHTS INTO THE VALUES AND THE RESULTING BEHAVIOR PATTERNS OF THE "JAMES" AND "ALFRED" TYPES YOU HAVE OBSERVED THIS WEEK:

THE "JAMES TYPE" OBSERVED:

THE "ALFRED TYPE" OBSERVED:

CONCLUSIONS:

Name _____

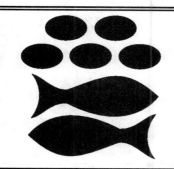

DAILY GROWTH GUIDE

THE FATHER'S SINGLE REQUEST

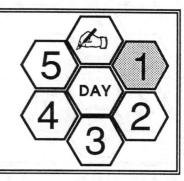

DAY ONE: WHAT IS GOD'S WILL FOR US?
SCRIPTURE READING: II PETER 3:9

1. Here is a classic verse which describes the will of God!
What is God **not** willing for men to do?

What is God willing for men to do?

2. How strongly have you been committed to what God wills, as stated in this verse?

☐ Strongly ☐ Mildly ☐ Very little

3. How strongly is your church committed to what God wills, as stated in this verse?

☐ Strongly ☐ Mildly ☐ Very little

4. Reflect on John 3:16 for a moment. Then answer the questions below:
What did God will for His "only begotten Son?"

What about the "adopted sons?" Are they without knowledge of His will for them?

What change in your own lifestyle would have to take place to do His will?

> *THOUGHT FOR THE DAY:*
> *AS GOD'S ADOPTED CHILDREN, WE ARE FREE TO ENJOY THE BEST POSSIBLE LIFESTYLE. THAT WILL MEAN PARTICIPATION IN OUR FATHER'S WORK. GOD'S ACTIVITY IS TO ADOPT ALL OF ADAM'S CHILDREN. THEREFORE, THE BEST POSSIBLE LIFESTYLE MAKES THIS OUR FIRST PRIORITY, TOO!*

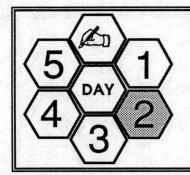
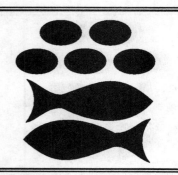
DAY TWO: WHAT COULD BE CLEARER?
SCRIPTURE READING: MATTHEW 28:18-20

In your opinion, what priority should be given to these eleven activities? Write a "1" beside the activity which should be given FIRST priority. Then, number all the rest, with "11" receiving the lowest priority.

PRIORITY
NUMBER

___ Worshipping

___ Working with Children

___ Belonging to a Group

___ Praying

___ Studying the Bible

___ Baptizing New Christians

PRIORITY
NUMBER

___ Singing in a Choir

___ Assisting Those In Crisis Situations

___ Bringing Unbelievers to Christ

___ Teaching Jesus' Commandments

___ Working with Teenagers

(Don't read the comment printed upside down until you have finished)

Life is never richer than when lived by God's priorities! In Matthew 28: 18-20, Jesus listed our top three priorities: (1) Disciple all people; (2) Baptize them; (3) Teach them. **What could be clearer?** The most significant thing we can do is bring unbelievers to Christ. Our second priority is to baptize them. The third is to teach them what Jesus has commanded. **Everything on our list must be under those priorities. If** God's wisdom is greater than ours (and it is!), then we are not getting the most out of life when we tamper with His priorities.

Did you get them in the proper order? Congratulations! You are among 3-5% of those who got it right on the first try. Most of those who have completed this exercise rate "Bringing Unbelievers to Christ" among the **last four on the list!** Hendrick Kraemer says that most Christians consider church activities as the end of their service for Christ. Sad, sad...but true!

*THOUGHT FOR THE DAY:
GOD'S WILL IS NEITHER COMPLICATED NOR MYSTERIOUS. HIS WILL IS THAT EVERY PERSON ON THIS PLANET BE GIVEN THE OPPORTUNITY TO BE ADOPTED BY HIM. HIS REQUEST TO US IS VERY, VERY CLEAR: WE ARE TO BE THE ONES WHO SHARE THAT NEWS. FOR THE CHILDREN OF ADAM, IT IS "GOOD NEWS." WHY DO WE FEAR SHARING IT?*

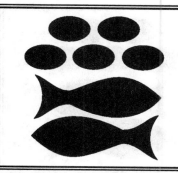

DAILY GROWTH GUIDE

THE FATHER'S SINGLE REQUEST

DAY THREE: WHAT IS AN "ADMINISTRATOR"?

SCRIPTURE READING: LUKE 12:42

Do you know what the Bible teaches about an "administrator?"
An "administrator" is a "steward," a household servant. He is charged to use the wealth of his master to meet the needs of the people who live in the household. As an "administrator," he does two things for those in the household:

1. He gives *proper rations...*
2. ... At the *proper time.*

1. **What do you enjoy the most?** (place an "X" by your answer)

☐ Giving gifts to others   ☐ Receiving gifts for myself

2. **Undoubtedly, you chose the first possibility. Why?**

3. **Have you ever wished *you* had enough wealth to present just the "right gift" to each person in your household at every "proper time" in their lives? If so, why did you have this desire?**

4. **Is today the "proper time" for someone to receive a "proper ration?"**

   WHO IS THAT PERSON?_____

5. **Do you believe God will supply to you what you need to give this person?**

☐ Yes   ☐ No   ☐ Not sure

THOUGHT FOR THE DAY:
BEING AN ADMINISTRATOR OF GOD'S SUPPLY IS THE MOST MEANINGFUL LIFE STYLE POSSIBLE FOR YOU! YOU CAN CONSTANTLY GIVE OUT THE PROPER RATION AT THE PROPER TIME TO EACH PERSON IN YOUR LIFE. A CONSTANT SUPPLY OF SPIRITUAL GIFTS ARE PROVIDED TO YOU BY YOUR LORD. YOUR GIFTS ARE GIVEN TO YOU SO YOU MIGHT BLESS OTHERS. GIVING THAT SUPPLY AWAY CAUSES YOU TO BECOME GOD'S "ADMINISTRATOR!"

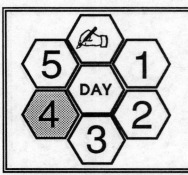

DAILY GROWTH GUIDE

THE FATHER'S SINGLE REQUEST

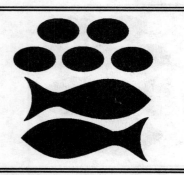

DAY FOUR: HOW DOES GOD WORK THROUGH MEN?

SCRIPTURE READING: ACTS 3:1-8; MATTHEW 28:18

1. **Why do you think the lame man was begging for money?**

   ☐ He felt nothing better could be received

   ☐ He had a great financial need at the time

   ☐ He did not dream anyone could help his lameness

2. **What reveals he had lived with this attitude for some time?** *(see verse 2)*

3. **Read what Peter said to him. Would you have said such words? Why or why not?**

4. **What provisions did God give to Peter, His "Administrator ?"**

   ☐ The same kind Adam's children possess

   ☐ Unique supernatural power

   ☐ The power of positive thinking

5. **What provision do you believe the "all power" in Matthew 28:18 gives to today's "Administrators ?"**

   ☐ The ability to encourage others with loving words

   ☐ The promise that in eternity things will be better than now

   ☐ The proper rations for the proper time

THOUGHT FOR THE DAY:
WE LACK GOD'S POWER BECAUSE WE HAVE NO NEED OF IT. WE HAVE NO NEED OF SUPERNATURAL PROVISIONS WHEN WE ARE NOT ADMINISTRATORS, DISPENSING "PROPER RATIONS AT THE PROPER TIME." THE MOST MEANINGFUL LIFESTYLE OF ALL IS LIKE BEING PLUGGED INTO AN ELECTRIC SOCKET: HIS CURRENT FLOWING THROUGH YOU!

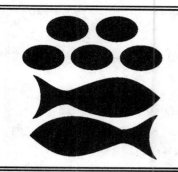

DAILY GROWTH GUIDE

THE FATHER'S SINGLE REQUEST

DAY FIVE: THE BEST LIFESTYLE POSSIBLE IS...

SCRIPTURE READING: LUKE 4:18-19

"As the Father has sent Me, so send I you." These words of Jesus make it clear that Luke 4:18-19 is not only His lifestyle. It is ours as well! The six ministries Jesus mentions are paraphrased below. Draw lines from each one to actions which are appropriate to them:

PROCLAIM GOOD NEWS TO THE POOR

Show gentleness to a nasty person

Help a young adult face the sin involved in a sexual liaison

PROVIDE HEALING FOR THE BROKENHEARTED

Take an unbeliever to visit a Share Group with you

Provide financial assistance to a friend who lost his job

ANNOUNCE RELEASE (PARDON) TO PRISONERS

Spend an evening with a friend whose husband has left her for another woman

RECOVERING OF SIGHT TO THE BLIND

Share your conversion story

Tell a zit-faced teenager he's so significant that God wants to adopt him

SET FREE THE BRUISED

Invite a friend to accept Christ as Lord

Pray with a friend facing surgery

ANNOUNCE THE TIME HAS COME WHEN OUR LORD WILL ACCEPT ALL MEN

Help a depressed friend get a new grasp on life

THOUGHT FOR THE DAY:
ADAM'S CHILDREN SEEK SIGNIFICANCE THROUGH LIFESTYLES DEVOTED TO POWER, POSSESSIONS, OR PLEASURE. WITH THEIR SIGNIFICANCE ASSURED BY ADOPTION, GOD'S CHILDREN CHOOSE INSTEAD TO BE ADMINISTRATORS OF GOD'S RESOURCES. THEIR LIFESTYLE PROVIDES THEM WITH A FAR GREATER HAPPINESS. ..AND BRINGS NEW LIFE TO OTHERS!

Thought For The Week

People with responsibility are in danger of throwing up barriers between themselves and those for whom they are responsible. They give the impression of always being busy...These leaders are afraid and create fear in others. They keep their distance because they are insecure. Truly responsible people are open to others...walking gives others a chance to meet them and talk to them like friends. They do not hide in their offices, and so stay vulnerable to criticism. People in authority should always stay close to those for whom they are responsible and encourage true and simple meetings. If they stay aloof, they cannot know their people or their people's needs.

It is important for people in authority to reveal themselves as they are and share their difficulties and weaknesses. If they hide these, people may see them as an unattainable model. They have to be seen as fallible and human, but at the same time trusting and trying to grow.

•Jean Vanier, in *Community and Growth*

Sitting down, Jesus called the Twelve and said, "If anyone wants to be first, he must be the very last, and the servant of all." He took a little child and had him stand among them. Taking him in his arms, he said to them, "Whoever welcomes one of these little children in my name welcomes me; and whoever welcomes me does not welcome me but the one who sent me."

• *Mark 9:36-37*

3

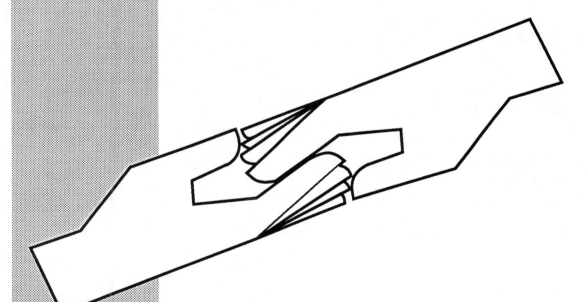

IS WHAT WE DO
THE RESULT OF
WHO WE ARE?

PERSONAL INVENTORY

Just before watching the videotape, thoughtfully answer these questions...

	AGREE	UNCERTAIN	DISAGREE
Since my significance stems from my adoption, developing my talents and gifts is unimportant.	☐	☐	☐
I am enjoying all the rights that are mine as a child of God.	☐	☐	☐
There is no significant difference between my values and those of my non-Christian friends.	☐	☐	☐
Some of my non-Christian friends seem to have a much happier life than I do.	☐	☐	☐
If I waste my gifts and talents, my significance becomes less to God.	☐	☐	☐
God doesn't care what I do with my talents and abilities.	☐	☐	☐
I am more significant to God when I do not commit serious sin.	☐	☐	☐
God sees me as a more significant person because I am taking this course.	☐	☐	☐
I feel a closer relationship to God when I think of all He has provided for me.	☐	☐	☐
If God were to allow great suffering to come to me or my family, I would reject Him.	☐	☐	☐

VIDEO PRESENTATION

Divide the Outline among the group members to review after video is viewed.

IS WHAT WE DO THE RESULT OF WHO WE ARE?

1. **LIFE'S FIRST TWO BASIC PRINCIPLES**
   A. Our significance comes from who we are, not what we do
      1. Adoption by God makes us eternally significant
      2. We're free from the pressure to prove we are significant
      3. Now, we can do significant things for the proper reasons
   B. The significance of what we do results from who we are

2. **THE FURTHER HISTORY OF ALFRED**
   A. His inner civil war
      1. Conflicting values with those of the Father
      2. Desire to pull away from His influence
   B. His proposal to the Father
      1. Refusal of Administrator's role
      2. Request for his inheritance...*in advance!*
   C. The Father's response

3. **ALFRED'S LIFE AWAY FROM THE FATHER**
   A. His initial "success"
      1. Possessions: the best available
      2. Relationships: lots of action
      3. Esteem: his money bought much respect
   B. His gradual disintegration
      1. Relationships dissolve into vapor
      2. Inner loss of meaning

4. **ALFRED'S RETURN TO THE FATHER'S HOUSE**
   A. His request to be a servant
   B. The Father's refusal; restored to sonship
   C. James' anger vented toward him
   D. The Father's pointed evaluations
   E. Both sons see their self-centered life styles

5. **TWO SONS FACE THEIR OWN REFLECTIONS**
   A. Alfred, broken, seeks his Father's forgiveness
   B. James, uprooted, sees his pride as an ugly thing
      1. He admits his love for the Father is shallow
      2. He makes a decision to reject this dark side of himself

6. **NEW RELATIONSHIPS WITH THE FATHER ESTABLISHED**
   A. Alfred finds a new beginning in the Father's presence
   B. James invades their love feast with his confession
   C. For the first time, both sons desire the Father's will

DISCUSSION TOPICS

Always begin with your DAILY REPORT TIME
Let each person share briefly;
report insights gained by completing
the Weekly Assignment.

STATEMENTS TO DISCUSS

1. Overcontrol keeps people from becoming responsible for their choices. Knowing that, would you have treated Alfred as the Father did? Why, or why not?

2. Alfred would probably never have changed if his values had not been tested to the limit. It is when we press our own values to the limit that we discover whether they are valid or not. Sad, but true...much of the wreckage in our life has resulted from learning lessons the hard way.

3. It takes about five resounding failures to shake false values out of our lifestyle. Each one brings us to see that God's plan for our life is really more beautiful than our own schemes for living.

DIG A LITTLE DEEPER THIS TIME...

...CONCERNING THE "JAMES" TYPES:

If they do not give themselves to reaching unbelievers, what *do* they give themselves to? Do they substitute tithing for personal involvement with others? Do they ever give with abandonment, or always guardedly? Do they carefully control their assets? Does this reveal limited understanding of Christ's Lordship in their lives?

Examine the friends they have chosen: what types of people do they value being around? What types have no significance to them? Do they carefully select only certain "classes" of people? (For example, other Christians like themselves?) Are their OIKOSES* purposely empty of unbelievers? Is this quite deliberate? Are they conscious of the needs of others?

From what do they gain satisfaction? If serving others is not meaningful, what substitute have they found? Last week you observed this point in Alfred's life. What similarities are there between the two types? How do they differ?

...CONCERNING THE "ALFRED" TYPES:

What value does money have to those you have observed? What about the value of time? Are these two commodities carefully protected, their value fully respected? Or, are they thoughtlessly used?

Do they live in the present only? Do they think of the future? Does "tomorrow" have any reality for them?

The accomplishments that give them the greatest pleasure indicate their view of success. What, in their minds, is "success?"

---

*Circle of close friends, family, etc.

PRACTICAL ASSIGNMENT

YOU CONTINUED YOUR OBSERVATIONS OF THE "JAMES TYPES" AND THE "ALFRED TYPES." WHAT NEW INSIGHTS HAVE YOU GAINED?

...FROM OBSERVING THE "JAMES TYPES:"

...FROM OBSERVING THE "ALFRED TYPES:"

CONCLUSIONS:

Name _____

DAILY GROWTH GUIDE

WE DO
WHAT WE ARE

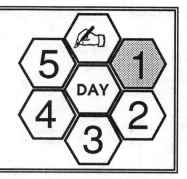

5 DAY 1
4 2
3

DAY ONE: THE CHARACTER OF A PRODIGAL
SCRIPTURE READING: LUKE 15: 11-32

1. **Whose story is recorded here?** ☐ Alfred's   ☐ James'

2. **Which statement properly links the son's values with those of some Christians?** (Please circle one of the following letters)

   A. He was a son who wanted his own will to be done.

   B. He was totally convinced his own will was "best."

   C. Both of the above.

   D. Neither of the above.

3. **Why was the son so blind to the foolishness of his choices?**
   (Arrange the comments below in the order of their priority.
   Place a "1" by your first choice, a "2" by your second, etc.)

   ____ He wanted to be accepted by his friends at all costs.

   ____ He was basically selfish at the center of his being.

   ____ He desired to have power, to be in control of others.

   ____ He was essentially insensitive to any needs except his own.

4. **Why did the father sacrifice his wealth to satisfy the whims of his son?**

   ☐ He had spoiled the son, and could no longer control him.

   ☐ He believed the cost was worth the lesson the son would learn.

THOUGHT FOR THE DAY:
WHERE DOES ALFRED LIVE? WITHIN EACH ONE OF US! BEING SELF-CENTERED, TRUSTING IN MYSELF RATHER THAN THE FATHER, IS A CHARACTER TRAIT WITHIN ALL OF ADAM'S CHILDREN. WE DO WHAT WE ARE. WE'LL NEVER DO ANYTHING DIFFERENTLY UNTIL WE ARE DIFFERENT. BEING COMES BEFORE DOING!

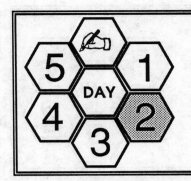

DAILY GROWTH GUIDE

WE DO
WHAT WE ARE

DAY TWO: THE VALUES OF A PRODIGAL
SCRIPTURE READING: LUKE 15:12

1. In two sentences, describe the character of the younger son:

2. What did he want from his father?

3. What did he receive from his father?

4. List three things that, in your opinion, the younger son missed receiving from his father because of his attitude and actions?

    1.

    2.

    3.

5. Many Christians, while living good, clean lives, never bother with others, and never share their faith. In your opinion, what does it cost them to live like that?

THOUGHT FOR THE DAY:
ALFRED IS AN AWFUL REMINDER OF A SAD TRUTH...IT IS TRAGICALLY POSSIBLE TO BE THE FATHER'S CHILD, YET POSSESS A LOST LIFE. HOW LOST TO A LIFE OF SERVICE ARE...YOU? ONE NEED NOT GO TO A "FAR CITY" TO TAKE ALL GOD HAS GIVEN, YET GIVE HIM NOTHING BACK...

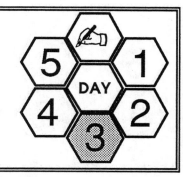
DAY THREE: THE DISILLUSIONMENT OF A PRODIGAL

SCRIPTURE READING: LUKE 15:13-16

1. **What does this passage show us about the importance of right choices in our lives?**

2. **The son's unlimited freedom revealed what his values would do to him. In verses 13 and 14, what values are revealed by his conduct?**
   (Check only the correct answers)

   ☐ Personal independence

   ☐ Making a good impression

   ☐ Satisfaction of physical lust

   ☐ Ignorance of true worth of wealth

   ☐ Live for today, not tomorrow

   (All of the above are correct answers!)

3. **This son's freedom was not restricted by his father. In your opinion, what does this reveal about the freedom God gives to us?**

4. **Is it true that every seed sown must be eventually reaped?**

THOUGHT FOR THE DAY:
FREEDOM IS A DANGEROUS THING! IT ALLOWS OUR VALUE SYSTEM TO TAKE US TO AN INEVITABLE DESTINATION. BEING FREE TO DO AS WE CHOOSE REVEALS MANY THINGS ABOUT OURSELVES WE MIGHT NEVER KNOW OTHERWISE. WITHOUT FREEDOM, WE NEVER GROW. BUT WHEN WE HAVE FREEDOM TO CHOOSE, WE PAY FOR OUR WRONG CHOICES.

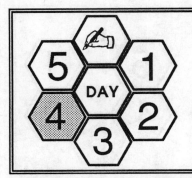

DAY FOUR: THE RETURN OF A PRODIGAL
SCRIPTURE READING: LUKE 15:17-32

1. How had the younger son's actions changed his relationship with his father?

A. From the son's viewpoint:

B. From the father's viewpoint:

2. How do our actions change our relationship with our Heavenly Father?

A. From our viewpoint:

B. From the Father's viewpoint:

3. Why do you think the son had the courage to return home?

☐ He figured his father was a "soft touch"

☐ He was confident of his father's unchanging love

☐ It was worth a try before going in another direction

*THOUGHT FOR THE DAY:
THE FATHER IS AMAZING. WRONG CHOICES DID NOT LEAD TO
ACCUSATION. RIGHT CHOICES BROUGHT CELEBRATION. THE SON'S
ABUSE OF HIS FATHER'S LOVE DID NOT DESTROY THE RELATIONSHIP.
SIN'S WORST, BROUGHT TO GOD, IS NO MATCH FOR HIS GRACE!*

DAILY GROWTH GUIDE

WE DO
WHAT WE ARE

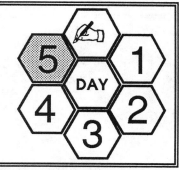

DAY FIVE: GOD'S RESPONSE TO A PERSON WHO REPENTS
SCRIPTURE READING: LUKE 15:7

> *"Repent:"* To turn around and walk in the opposite direction.

1. Jesus made this statement before introducing the story of the prodigal son. How does the story illustrate this statement?

2. In your opinion, why is there so much joy in Heaven when a sinner repents?

3. What are your feelings when you observe a sinner repenting?
   (Check closest answer to your own feelings)

   ☐ Detached, objective

   ☐ Skeptical about the sincerity of the person

   ☐ Fills me with deep emotion, even to the point of tears

   ☐ Makes me want to encourage others to repent

4. Do you have a deep desire to touch others with your life, bringing them to repentance? Why or why not?

THOUGHT FOR THE DAY:
WHAT ARE WE SO SHALLOW IN OUR THINKING? IF ALL HEAVEN SINGS WITH JOY WHEN JUST ONE PERSON COMES TO THE FATHER, WHY DO WE CARE SO LITTLE ABOUT IT? WHAT ABOUT THE FIRST NON-CHRISTIAN WHO WILL MEET YOU AFTER YOU FINISH THIS PAGE? IF YOU FAIL TO SHARE YOUR FAITH, WILL ANYONE ELSE DO IT FOR YOU?

Thought For The Week

Who is more tragic than Alfred?

It's a sad thing to see a son of Adam wasting his life away, committed to tiny goals which leave nothing of worth behind. It's a shatteringly sad thing to see a *son of God* doing the same thing!

The really potent thing about the story of the Prodigal Son is that he *was a son.* But, is Alfred the *only* prodigal? Is not James just as disobedient to the will of his Father, but in a more quiet way?

We look about the church of today and ask, "Who is the prodigal child of God in our generation?"

The answer is one we may not wish to hear: Today's prodigal is the deacon who tithes and even works around the church, but refuses to wash feet as a true "servant" must. Today's prodigal is the busy, busy, *busy* church worker who ignores human suffering in the home next door and the alcoholic who lives across the street.

Today's prodigal is the church member who has equalized Sunday worship, holidays, and family traditions as "proper" for all civilized people.

The prodigals of today are those Christians who visit the church property once a week to be sure it has not been vandalized between Sundays, and who use the worship hour to plan the coming week's activities. It is the person who gives a pittance to the work of God, but owns a second home, or a boat, or an expensive car. It is important that, as Christians, we learn that we must live simply in order that others may simply live.

The prodigal is the Christian who has not yet learned that God's children deliberately choose to become responsible for what they are *not* responsible for, and that they are their brother's keeper.

What God is waiting for is brokenness among the prodigals. When our values are clarified and we begin to love with His love, we will see a new church in our world. Oh, God! How long must we wait?

But they kept silent, for on the way they had discussed with one another which of them was the greatest. And sitting down, He called the twelve and said to them, "If anyone wants to be first, he shall be last of all, and servant of all."

• *Mark 9:34-35*

38

4

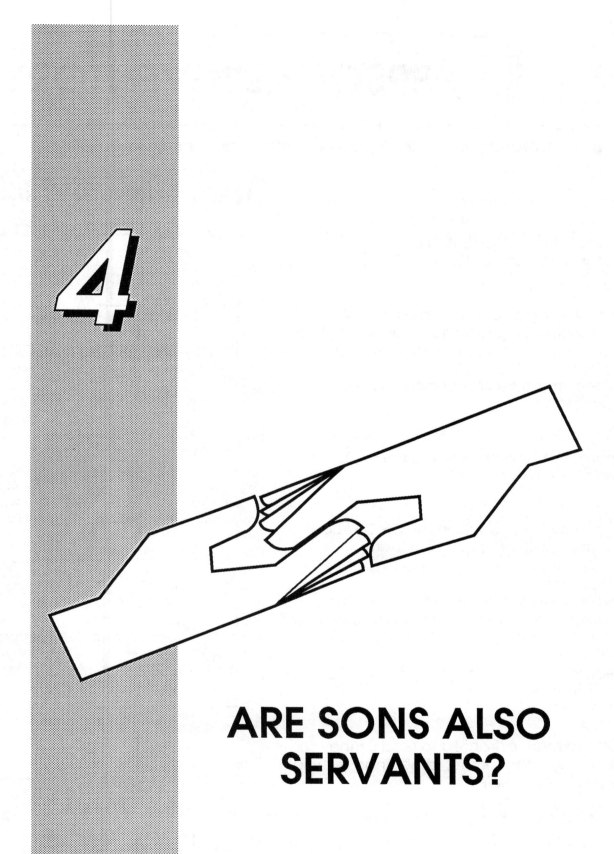

ARE SONS ALSO SERVANTS?

PERSONAL INVENTORY

Just before watching the videotape, thoughtfully answer these questions...

	AGREE	UNCERTAIN	DISAGREE
Jesus was more important to God as a Son than as a Servant	☐	☐	☐
I can choose to become a child of God without ever facing the choice of serving Him	☐	☐	☐
I can become a serving person, even as was Jesus	☐	☐	☐
The disciples became servants from following the example of Jesus	☐	☐	☐
There are certain people in my OIKOS I can only reach for Christ by serving them	☐	☐	☐
If I become a servant, I need to maintain enough control of my life to take care of myself	☐	☐	☐
If I become a servant, I will have to give away all my resources	☐	☐	☐
Others are more attracted to God as they see what he has done for me, rather than by what I have made of myself	☐	☐	☐
Servanthood is optional for Christians	☐	☐	☐
I should become a servant because God wants me to do so	☐	☐	☐

VIDEO PRESENTATION

Divide the Outline between the group members to review after video is viewed.

ARE SONS ALSO SERVANTS?

1. *PAIS:* **A FAMILY WORD**
   A. Translated "child," or "son"
      1. Matthew 17:18
      2. In King James, "child"
      3. In New American Standard Version, "son"
   B. Used to describe a **relationship**

2. *PAIS:* **A SERVANT WORD**
   A. Translated "servant"
      1. Matthew 14:1-2
      2. Used here exclusively as "servant"
   B. To be a SON is to be a SERVANT
      1. Acts 3:13, 26; 4:27, 30
      2. Interchangeably "son" and "servant"
   C. Isaiah 42:1 and Matthew 12:18

3. **SONSHIP MAKES US SERVANTS**
   A. Jesus, God's only begotten Son, was a Servant
      1. His own claim: Luke 22:27, Matthew 20:28
      2. His very **nature** was that of a servant
      3. What He did was the result of who He was
   B. His very nature has been placed within us
      1. I John 4:13-17
      2. His Spirit inside us will cause us to be servants

4. **A NORMAL CHRISTIAN IS A SERVANT OF GOD**
   A. Mark 9: Jesus confronts His disciples with this fact
   B. Verse 36: We serve without expecting rewards
   C. Our service is the result of a **relationship**
   D. Illustration: Mayor's chauffeur in Seoul, Korea
   E. Who do we serve? **ALL**

5. **THE IMPORTANCE OF OUR BEING GOD'S SERVANTS**
   A. **Only** the adopted can explain what adoption is like
   B. Adam's children need their conception of God changed
      1. They view Him as a powerful ruler
      2. In fact, our God has a servant heart of love

6. **THE SIGNIFICANCE OF BEING GOD'S SERVANT**
   A. We are free from the pressure of "winning" and "losing"
   B. As a son, not a servant, I reject being my own master
   C. My greatest joy comes from relating to God and His work

DISCUSSION TOPICS

Always begin with your DAILY REPORT TIME
Let each person share briefly;
report insights gained by completing
the Practical Assignment.

DAILY REPORT TIME: (10 minutes) Let each person share for no more than one minute, reporting insights gained from the Weekly Assignment. Then use the remaining portion of the 10 minutes for a general discussion of your findings.

Small Group Discussion (20 Minutes)

THINGS I DO...	...WHAT I AM
1.	
2.	
3.	
THINGS I WANT TO DO...	**...WHAT I WOULD BE**
4.	
5.	
6.	

List in the first three lines above 3 things you do, over and over and over! In the next column, write down what they signify you are.

Then, on the next three lines, add 3 things you would like to add to your list, and what they would signify you are.

Finally, cross out any of the first three you wish to eliminate from your lifestyle.

Share your report in about two minutes with the group. Use the final 10 minutes for general discussion.

You will be observing a totally different lifestyle this week. If your church is small or medium in size, it is possible that several in your group will select the same persons to observe. Why? Has your church life produced many of these types of persons? If not, why? If so, how did it happen?

QUESTIONS TO GUIDE YOU...

What periods of time does this person reserve for private fellowship with the Father? How is that time used? Is it a daily time, or what pattern does it follow?

How "real" is God to this person? Is there a true communion with Him, or is it more a formal awareness of His presence?

What is this person's belief about eternity? Does it exist? Do we live forever? Is there a conscious valuing of the temporary versus the eternal?

Why is this person significantly different from Alfred and James? What accomplishments give him the greatest pleasure? What persons and things are valued the most?

How does this person view wealth? Does he view himself as an Administrator of his possessions, rather than the owner of them?

What is different about this person that causes his friendships to contain a significant number of unbelievers? What inner values are reflected by this fact?

How does this person find time to be involved in church activities and minister to Adam's children at the same time? Do you perceive there is a deliberate limitation set upon his use of time, which makes *ministry* possible?

INSIGHTS AND OBSERVATIONS FROM THE
PRACTICAL ASSIGNMENT

WHAT VALUES DID YOU YOU OBSERVE IN THE TWO "SON-SERVANTS"
YOU WATCHED THIS WEEK?
• LIST FOUR OF THEM.
• THEN, UNDERLINE THE ONE WHICH IMPRESSED YOU THE MOST:

1.

2.

3.

4.

WHAT CONTRASTS IN VALUES AND LIFESTYLES DID YOU FIND BETWEEN
THESE TWO PERSONS AND THE "JAMES TYPES" AND "ALFRED TYPES" YOU
HAVE PREVIOUSLY OBSERVED?

_____
Name

DAILY GROWTH GUIDE

SERVANTHOOD IS NOT OPTIONAL

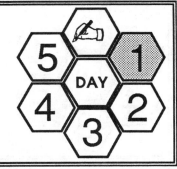

DAY ONE: AN OPPORTUNITY TO BECOME RESPONSIBLE
SCRIPTURE READING: MATTHEW 10:1, 16-23

1. **Would you like for Jesus to give you the same power He gave His disciples in Matthew 10:1?**

   ☐ "I'd welcome it!"

   ☐ "I would accept it, knowing the responsibility of it would change my lifestyle in a radical way."

   ☐ "I don't believe it's possible, so I can't answer the question."

   ☐ "I don't want it. It would demand more than I wish to give to others."

2. **With power came responsibility. What was the result of receiving this power, as recorded in verses 16-23?**
   (Answer in just a sentence or two)

3. **As the adopted sons of God, Jesus says to us: "All power is given to me...Behold, I am with you" (Matthew 28:18-20). In your opinion, what responsibility is included with the promise of this power?**
   (No "multiple choice" for you. Do some straight thinking.)

THOUGHT FOR THE DAY:
POWER IS NOT ENTRUSTED TO THOSE WHO ARE CARELESS IN THE USE IF IT. PERHAPS THAT EXPLAINS WHY SO FEW CHRISTIANS ARE ENTRUSTED WITH THE POWER OF GOD. POWER IS THE TWIN SISTER OF PURITY. SOME THINK THEY WANT MORE POWER, WHEN IT IS PURITY THEY NEED.

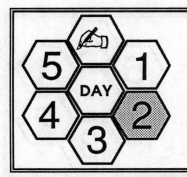

DAILY GROWTH GUIDE

SERVANTHOOD IS NOT OPTIONAL

DAY TWO: HOW WILL THEY HEAR?
SCRIPTURE READING: MATTHEW 10: 6-7; ISAIAH 53:6

1. Jesus sent his twelve disciples to "lost sheep." Which of these statements describe this condition?

☐ They walked a carefully wrapped pathway

☐ They were bewildered about what direction to take

☐ They were wasting precious days, lived without purpose

☐ They were without a shepherd to guide them

2. What was the message the disciples were to bring? (verse 7)

3. The "kingdom of Heaven" means: "The time during which God reigns." Why would that message be attractive to "lost sheep?"

☐ Because it will comfort them while they wander around

☐ Because they will know road signs will soon be installed

☐ Because, in reigning, God will direct and guide them

4. According to Isaiah 53:6, when we are lost, which way do we turn?

5. Why is it almost a criminal act to have such news to share with lost sheep...and to withhold it?

THOUGHT FOR THE DAY:
A MAN CANNOT TOUCH HIS NEIGHBOR'S HEART WITH ANYTHING LESS THAN HIS OWN.

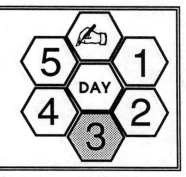
DAY THREE: HOW DO WE SPEAK?
SCRIPTURE READING: MATTHEW 10:8-10

1. **List what the disciples were to do, and were not to do:**

To Do	Not To Do
1.	1.
2.	2.
3.	3.
4.	4.
5.	

2. **Why do both the "Do's" and the "Don't Do's" point to a total dependence upon God's power, rather than our own?**

3. **Why do you think they were instructed to use God's resources to meet physical needs, rather than to focus only on spiritual needs?**

THOUGHT FOR THE DAY:
THE WAY TO REACH A PERSON IS TO SERVE HIM, AND OUR SERVICE IS RELATED TO NEEDS. IF GOD CANNOT MEET THOSE NEEDS, WHY WOULD A PERSON WANT TO BE ADOPTED BY HIM? WE ARE NOT TO GO IN WORDS BUT IN DEEDS, MEETING NEEDS.

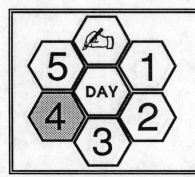

DAILY GROWTH GUIDE

SERVANTHOOD
IS NOT OPTIONAL

DAY FOUR: WHERE SHALL WE MINISTER?
SCRIPTURE READING: LUKE 9:1-4

1. **The word "house" is our old friend, "*OIKOS!*" The word "abide" means to "stay a long time." Why were the disciples told to penetrate just one *oikos* and remain in it?** (check one)

   ☐ It was important to become a solid citizen in the community.

   ☐ When one lives in an *oikos*, others can observe the integrity of one's life.

   ☐ It saved money to stay in one spot, rather than moving around.

2. **What does this teach us about our responsibility to our own *oikos*?**

3. **Why does it take time to penetrate the life and values of another person?** (check all answers you consider correct)

   ☐ People do not rely heavily on quick, first impressions.

   ☐ Different values emerge in different situations. Being around someone else for a period of time fully reveals most of their values.

   ☐ One needs to "wear down" another person's resistance by persistence.

THOUGHT FOR THE DAY:
MINISTRY USUALLY TAKES MORE TIME THAN WE EXPECT. WHEN WE TRY TO JUMP IN AND OUT OF MINISTERING TO OTHERS, FEW RESULTS WILL BE GAINED. SERVING OTHERS REQUIRES TIME...TO SEE SEEDS PLANTED RIPEN INTO HARVESTABLE FRUIT.

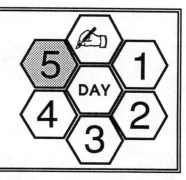
DAY FIVE: SERVANTS BRING PEACE
SCRIPTURE READING: MATTHEW 10:12-1

1. What do these verses tell us about the result the disciples could expect?

2. How would you rephrase the term "greeting of peace," used in this verse?

3. What defense mechanisms do you usually use in a situation where you may have to face rejection?

   ☐ Avoid the discussion in the first place.

   ☐ Sense the "danger zone," and agree with the other person's viewpoint.

   ☐ Share my convictions openly, but without forcing them on others.

   ☐ Argue until the other person has given in to my views.

4. Which of the above ways is proper to use in bringing a "greeting of peace" to those in our *oikos?*

THOUGHT FOR THE DAY:
WE ARE NOT GOING TO BE WELCOMED BY ALL, AND YET WHEREVER WE GO PEACE CAN COME. THE TRAGEDY IS THE WAY WE PREOCCUPY OURSELVES WITH RELIGIOUS ACTIVITY INSTEAD OF MINISTRY.

Thought For The Week

It's a lot safer topic to think about God's love for us than to think about our love for Him. The true statement of our love for Him is not the amount of time we spend in our "prayer closet" talking to Him, or the hours we spend memorizing scripture. Our love is indicated by our participation in His heart's desire...and that is clearly stated in the scripture. He is not willing that ANY should perish.

For that reason, He gave His only begotten Son. For that reason, He does not take every adopted Son home to be with Him at the moment of conversion. He leaves us here for a precise mission. As stewards, we are to give "proper rations at the proper time" to those in our *oikos.*

Oh, that our generation of believers would consider it an act of unspeakable treason for us to "sit and soak" every Sunday in church services, while our own neighbors live in the emptiness of unbelief! Those who live in TOUCH with us are not going to be reached until we become servant people to them. They are tired of high-pressured "sales pitches" in the name of Christ. They ache to see the reality of an invisible God shaping the spirit, the heart, the conduct, the use of wealth, the *everything,* of Christians. This, and this alone, will bring them to the Master.

What would it take for this truth to penetrate your life to the fullest...to come to that point where you would say, as martyred missionary Jim Elliot said, *"HE IS NO FOOL WHO GIVES WHAT HE CANNOT KEEP TO GAIN WHAT HE CANNOT LOSE"*

"Greater love has no one than this, that one lay down his life for his friends"
• John 15:13

5

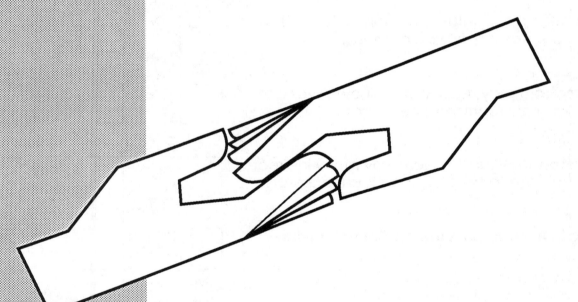

WHAT MAKES
SERVING SO
SIGNIFICANT?

PERSONAL INVENTORY

Just before watching the videotape, thoughtfully answer these questions...

	AGREE	UNCERTAIN	DISAGREE
I can have as strong a relationship with God by being His child as being His servant	☐	☐	☐
God does not care if I ignore His call to minister to Adam's children if I stay busy in some other church activity	☐	☐	☐
Involvement in the Father's mission to Adam's children creates a special closeness to Him	☐	☐	☐
Christians who play master of their own lives do not adequately represent the Father	☐	☐	☐
We can reach Adam's children by many indirect methods. Face to face contact is unnecessary!	☐	☐	☐
Working in my church is the end of my service for the Lord	☐	☐	☐
People who are not Christians are hard to reach, and only experts should attempt it	☐	☐	☐
Skepticism about God and Jesus among the children of Adam can be answered by serving them	☐	☐	☐
Endless, non-servant activity makes some people become radiant, joyful Christians	☐	☐	☐
Christians who do not serve are like a very cold, heated room: A total contradiction!	☐	☐	☐

VIDEO PRESENTATION

Divide the Outline among the group members to review after video is viewed.

WHAT MAKES SERVING SO SIGNIFICANT?

1. **REVIEW**
   A. Principles Learned Thus Far:
      1. Our Significance: who we are, not what we do
      2. What we do the result of who we are
   B. Five things to remember:
      1. The spirit of a servant has been born in me
      2. Being a child and a servant are both relationships
      3. Being master destroys servant relationship
      4. Servant life required to reveal God's character
      5. With God, there are no little people

2. **SERVING IS THE MOST SIGNIFICANT THING IN MY LIFE**
   A. The Father probes for information
      1. He asks about bitterness in their hearts
      2. Both reassure him it has finally been removed
   B. The Father encourages them to become Administrators
      1. James worries about whether Adam's children will respond
      2. The Father tells them of His natural Son's strategy
   C. James seeks the "easy way" out
      1. He proposes a non-servant assignment
      2. It is refused: a servant relationship is necessary!

3. **THE IMPACT OF SERVANT SONS UPON OTHERS**
   A. Alfred: among his friends in the city
      1. His relational life opens them to the Father's love
      2. His former partner asks to meet the Father
      3. A growing colony of adopted people established
   B. James: a different city, but the same objective
      1. Skepticism about the Father broken down by serving others
      2. His secretary the first one to be adopted

4. **SERVANTHOOD: OUR STRONGEST RELATIONSHIP WITH GOD**
   A. Working relationships bring a special closeness
      1. Intimacy with the Father is the most significant result
      2. Jesus: "No longer just **servants**, but **friends!**"
   B. It is estimated that only 15% of God's SONS are SERVANTS
   C. We cannot know Him by remaining in His house!
      1. Knowing His power is related to doing His work
      2. Without serving, we become hardened in religious life

5. **THE PEOPLE WITH THE PIERCED EARS**
   A. A symbol of voluntary servanthood
   B. A substitute for endless, non-servant activity
      1. Are you ready?
      2. If not, let's consider our alternatives...

DISCUSSION TOPICS

Always begin with your DAILY REPORT TIME Let each person share briefly; report insights gained by completing the Practical Assignment.

DAILY REPORT TIME: (10 minutes) Let each person share for no more than 1 minute, reporting insights gained from the Weekly Assignment. Then use the remaining portion of the 10 minutes for a general discussion of your findings.

GROUP ACTIVITY: (20 minutes)

As a group, list below five spiritual defects which may develop in Christians who continually stay "in the Lord's house," never serving the Children of Adam:

1.   4.

2.   5.

3.

What kind of "closeness" would be created between a Christian and the Lord by:

1. Working with a non-Christian couple with a marriage problem?

2. Getting groceries for a family whose breadwinner has been laid off?

3. Sharing the loneliness of a recently divorced parent?

4. Making friends with next door neighbors who are unchurched?

This is your PRACTICAL ASSIGNMENT for this coming week...

OBSERVE A CHRISTIAN WHO SEEMS TO SERVE ADAM'S CHILDREN TO A GREATER EXTENT THAN YOU PROBABLY DO. COMPARE YOUR OWN LIFESTYLES. IF POSSIBLE, CONTRAST THEIR FELLOWSHIP WITH THE FATHER WITH YOUR OWN. WHAT DIFFERENCES DO YOU SEE?

It's true! We will be essentially the same people five years from now, except for the **people we meet** and the **books or television programs we read or view.**

The weekly video presentations give you one view of servant life. Alfred and James are models of true-to-life types of people.

However, nothing can mean more to you than to compare your life, your values, your attitudes, and your activities, to a person who can serve as a "model" of a servant life. No matter where we are on our journey, there are always those who are behind us, and others who are beyond us, on the way. By looking to those who are beyond us, we get a little better idea of where we need to walk.

IT'S ALL A MATTER OF ATTITUDE!

Our attitudes reflect opinions of persons, places, and values. Dr. LeRoy Ford writes: "Values can change. A man previously blind said to Jesus, 'Whereas I was blind, now I see' (John 9:25). He meant not only physical blindness but also attitudinal blindness."

How do *our* attitudes change? By one of these four ways:

1. Observing leaders and friends who set the right example

2. Reading or hearing about persons who are examples

3. Confronting sources which give examples

4. Learning to identify servant characteristics

This is why you are asked to find someone beyond you on the journey, and to compare their lifestyle with your own. Sincerely seek to learn from this week's assignment. May God give you sensitivity as you do so.

55

PRACTICAL ASSIGNMENT

LIST BELOW YOUR CONCLUSIONS AFTER OBSERVING A CHRISTIAN WHO SEEMS TO SERVE ADAM'S CHILDREN TO A GREATER EXTENT THAN YOU PROBABLY DO.

WHAT DID YOU DISCOVER ABOUT THIS PERSON THAT YOU DID NOT KNOW BEFORE?

WHAT DID YOU LEARN ABOUT YOURSELF THAT YOU DID NOT KNOW BEFORE?

HOW IS THIS PERSON'S FELLOWSHIP WITH THE FATHER DEEPER BECAUSE OF A SERVANT LIFE?

Name _____

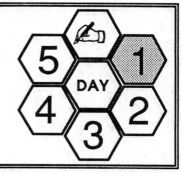
DAY ONE: A SPECIAL FRIENDSHIP WITH THE FATHER
SCRIPTURE READING: JOHN 16:24

1. **What special significance does this verse have for servants?**

2. **How do our prayers differ when we ask for our *own* needs, compared to asking for God's resources so we may serve *others*?**

3. **What special fellowship with the Father do we have when He provides such resources to serve others?**

THOUGHT FOR THE DAY:
"IF ALL YOU WANT TO DO IS WHAT GOD WANTS TO DO, YOU CAN DO WHATEVER YOU WANT TO DO!"

...Ian Thomas

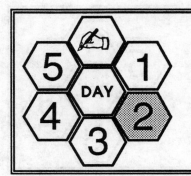

DAILY GROWTH GUIDE

*FRIENDSHIP:
THE SERVANT'S
REWARD*

DAY TWO: A SPECIAL FRIENDSHIP WITH JESUS
SCRIPTURE READING: JOHN 15:15-16

1. According to Jesus, what is the difference between a slave and a friend?

2. Why do friends know what the master does, when slaves will not?
(Check each answer you believe is true)

☐ Friends are more intelligent

☐ Friends are given reasons as well as orders

☐ Friends share in the task as partners with the master

☐ Slaves are not told the master's purpose...they are only given directions

3. Do you disagree, or agree, with this statement by Barclay? Why or why not?

"It is the tremendous choice that is laid out before us that we can accept or refuse partnership with Christ in the work of leading the world to God."
(Write your comment here)

*THOUGHT FOR THE DAY:
"THERE IS NOT AN INCH OF ANY SPHERE OF LIFE OVER WHICH JESUS
CHRIST DOES NOT SAY 'MINE' "*

...Abraham Kuyper

DAILY GROWTH GUIDE

FRIENDSHIP:
THE SERVANT'S
REWARD

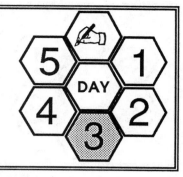

DAY THREE: A SPECIAL FRIENDSHIP WITH THE HOLY SPIRIT
SCRIPTURE READING: JOHN 15:26-27

1. How does John 14:26 take on a very special meaning for those who are not only God's adopted children, but who are also His servants?

2. According to John 15:26-27, what is the basis for the friendship which exists between the servant and the Holy Spirit?

3. The word "witness" means to "give evidence." Why do we feel especially close to the Holy Spirit when we are witnessing?

4. Can this same intimacy exist if a Christian is not a servant person?

THOUGHT FOR THE DAY:
O FOR A PASSIONATE PASSION FOR SOULS,
O FOR A PITY THAT YEARNS!
O FOR THE LOVE THAT LOVES UNTO DEATH,
O FOR THE FIRE THAT BURNS!
O FOR THE PURE PRAYER - PRAYER THAT PREVAILS,
THAT POURS ITSELF OUT FOR THE LOST!
VICTORIOUS PRAYER IN THE CONQUEROR'S NAME,
O FOR A PENTECOST!

...Amy Charmichael

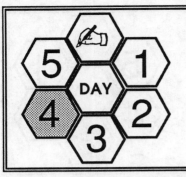

DAILY GROWTH GUIDE

FRIENDSHIP: THE SERVANT'S REWARD

DAY FOUR: A SPECIAL FRIENDSHIP WITH FELLOW SERVANTS
SCRIPTURE READING: COLOSSIANS 4:7-14

1. How many "Fellow Servants" does Paul identify in this short passage?

   ☐ Five ☐ Eight ☐ Twelve

2. What are the names of those identified as "servants" or "bondslaves?"

3. What sort of relationship do you sense existed among these men?

4. Why do you think that relationship existed?

5. Have you experienced this same kind of closeness with fellow Christians, as a result of serving the Lord together? Jot down their names, and something about the activity you shared:

THOUGHT FOR THE DAY:
"I DO NOT WANT PEOPLE WHO COME WITH ME UNDER CERTAIN RESERVATIONS. IN BATTLE YOU NEED SOLDIERS WHO FEAR NOTHING."

...Pere Didon

DAILY GROWTH GUIDE

FRIENDSHIP:
THE SERVANT'S
REWARD

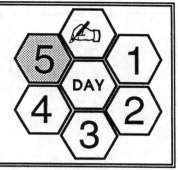

DAY FIVE: A SPECIAL FRIENDSHIP WITH ADAM'S CHILDREN
SCRIPTURE READING: ROMANS 10:13-15

1. **According to verse 13, what is the news we share with the children of Adam?**

2. **What is the result of our not becoming servant persons to them? (verse 14)**

3. **How do you connect the fact that we are "sent" into servanthood?**
   (Circle one of the following letters:)

   A. The decision to send us is made by the Master

   B. Preaching requires the authority of the Master

   C. Both of the above

   D. Neither of the above

THOUGHT FOR THE DAY:
"IF I LIE LOUNGING IN MY BED, WHILE OTHERS TOIL; THEN LET ME
STARVE, BE NEVER FED WITH HEAVENLY MANNA, HOLY BREAD, WHILE
PAIN AND SORROWS O'ER ME SPREAD - MY LIFE EMBROIL."
                                              ...R. E. Neighbour

Thought For The Week

So then, my brothers, because of God's great mercy to us I appeal to you: Offer yourselves as a living sacrifice to God, dedicated to his service and pleasing to him. This is the true worship that you should offer. Do not conform yourselves to the standards of this world, but let God transform you inwardly by a complete change of your mind. Then you will be able to know the will of God--what is good and is pleasing to Him and is perfect.

Romans 12:1-2 GNB

6

JESUS SPEAKS ABOUT

SERVANTHOOD

PERSONAL INVENTORY

Just before watching the videotape, thoughtfully answer these questions...

	AGREE	UNCERTAIN	DISAGREE
When I think of the disciples, I think of the finest Christians I know	☐	☐	☐
The disciples fully grasped the principles Jesus taught	☐	☐	☐
Leadership is being in control	☐	☐	☐
Promotions are very, very important to me	☐	☐	☐
I tend to respect people more if they are obviously at the top	☐	☐	☐
God is impressed by the status men attain	☐	☐	☐
Doing tough, hard jobs is for those who have not yet gained seniority in their business	☐	☐	☐
We are greatest when we are serving others	☐	☐	☐
I detest helping people who do not help back	☐	☐	☐
Happiness is the absence of pain	☐	☐	☐

VIDEO PRESENTATION

Divide the Outline among the group members to review after video is viewed.

JESUS SPEAKS ABOUT SERVANTHOOD

1. **HIS TEACHING AT THE TRANSFIGURATION**
   A. The value system of the disciples
      1. Desired to be great
      2. Expected Jesus to be another "Moses"
      3. Their argument over who would be greatest
   B. Jesus' teaching in Capernaum about servanthood

2. **HIS TEACHING ABOUT GREATNESS**
   A. Disciples try to manipulate Jesus
      1. James and John try to gain advantage
      2. Other disciples furious
   B. Jesus contrasts world's view with His own
      1. World: lord it over others
      2. God's way: must become servant of ALL
   C. Jesus uses Himself as an example

3. **HIS ACTIONS AT THE PASSOVER SUPPER**
   A. Disciples interested only in their status
      1. Jesus tells them one will betray Him
      2. They speculate about the "pecking order"
      3. They still aspire to greatness
   B. Jesus washes their feet
      1. Peter objects strenuously
      2. Jesus teaches them about servanthood again

4. **LIVING A SERVANT LIFE CHANGES OUR VIEWPOINT**
   A. Illustration: Pastor and Gangster
   B. Isaiah 52 & 53: Jesus' servant life predicted
   C. His greatness resulted from His servant life
   D. Greatness belongs to servants
   E. Servanthood is a matter of values, not status

DISCUSSION TOPICS

Always begin with your DAILY REPORT TIME
Let each person share briefly;
report insights gained by completing
the Practical Assignment.

DAILY REPORT TIME: (10 minutes) Let each person share for no more than 1 minute, reporting insights gained from the Weekly Assignment. Then use the remaining portion of the 10 minutes for a general discussion of your findings.

SMALL GROUP ACTIVITY: (20 minutes)

In the space below, write out a character sketch of your life as you would like to be in three years. (take 5 minutes to complete it)

In your group, read your character sketches to one another. Discuss the ways they reflect the principles of servanthood taught by Jesus to His disciples. (Use the last 15 minutes for this purpose)

WHEN, AND UNDER WHAT CIRCUMSTANCES, WILL YOUR LIFE BECOME MORE THAN IT IS AT THE PRESENT TIME?

One of the "blessings" that frequently occur when people are released from their employment, or when they move to a new location, is that they are free to disentangle themselves from habits of living. Too many of us continue to muddle along, never really entering a meaningful lifestyle...but not knowing how to go about changing it.

In the next weeks, your Weekly Assignment will be designed to help you take charge of your own existence, and to deliberately put into motion the principles of servanthood you have learned in LIFE BASIC TRAINING.

You will get **from** these assignments exactly what you put **into** them! You can work as hard as you want to, or slip through without much being done. It's really up to you. God has released each one of us to **choose** the servant life. When will you begin? How will you start? What about NOW? Turn the page...and begin to make deliberate decisions about your existence.

PRACTICAL ASSIGNMENT

IN THE SPACES BELOW, LIST TWELVE THINGS YOU WOULD LIKE TO EXPERIENCE, COMPLETE, OR UNDERTAKE IN YOUR LIFETIME. NONE OF THEM SHOULD HAVE ALREADY BEEN STARTED OR COMPLETED AT THIS TIME.

As you prepare your list, evaluate each item by asking: "How does this fit into God's purpose for my life as a servant person?" **Remember this principle:** "You can do anything you want to do, as long as you remain involved in sharing our Father's desire to adopt all the children of Adam." If there is any conflict between the things you list and that principle, you probably need to go back to the "Listening Room!"

1. _____

2. _____

3. _____

4. _____

5. _____

6. _____

7. _____

8. _____

9. _____

10. _____

11. _____

12. _____

Name _____

DAY ONE: THE VALUES OF JESUS: STATUS
SCRIPTURE READING: MATTHEW 20:25-28

1. **How do men assign status to each other? (verse 25)**

2. **Which person in the list below would gain prominence in the church, according to the way men assign status?**

   ☐ A widow who sews clothes for orphans

   ☐ A man who works with paroled prisoners

   ☐ A carpenter, who contributes sacrificially

   ☐ A man who is the President of Frabistats, Inc.

3. **According to verses 26-28, which person would have the highest status, valued in the manner Jesus assigns status?**

   ☐ A deacon, elected because he is wealthy and tithes

   ☐ A Sunday school teacher, admired for her great ability

   ☐ A pastor, selected because of his organizational skills

   ☐ A woman, who unsparingly ministers to pregnant teenagers

THOUGHT FOR THE DAY:
"Behold, thy King cometh unto thee, meek and sitting upon an ass, and a colt the foal of an ass." How absurd! What writer would do a scenario in which the Kind of the Jews, the Son of God, rides a young, staggering animal for a triumphal entry into a city? No other beast could make the powerful statement about the way Jesus considered status. His action completely ridiculed the way men impress other men. What a challenge to our value systems!

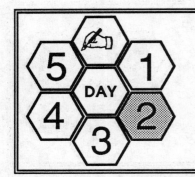

DAILY GROWTH GUIDE

THE VALUES OF JESUS

DAY TWO: THE VALUES OF JESUS: WEALTH
SCRIPTURE READING: MARK 14:3-7

One of the absurdities of our age is the idea that to be "spiritual" is to be poor. Our Father is the wealthiest landowner of all eternity! Should His children assume He wants them to be poor, while He is rich? Today's study may challenge some misconceptions you have...

1. **In this passage, how did those at Bethany value the perfume?**

   ☐ By its odor

   ☐ By its cost

   ☐ By its value if sold, and put to practical use

2. **How did the owner of the perfume assess its value?**

   ☐ By what she paid for it

   ☐ By how long she could enjoy it

   ☐ By the love she could show by anointing Jesus with it

3. **How did Jesus assess the value of it?**

   ☐ By the practical way it could help the poor

   ☐ By its use to display a deep love and devotion

4. **How should we consider the value of wealth?**

   ☐ By its buying power

   ☐ By its use in showing our love for Christ

   ☐ By the people who can be helped by it

THOUGHT FOR THE DAY:
YOU CAN GIVE WITHOUT LOVING, BUT YOU CANNOT LOVE WITHOUT GIVING!

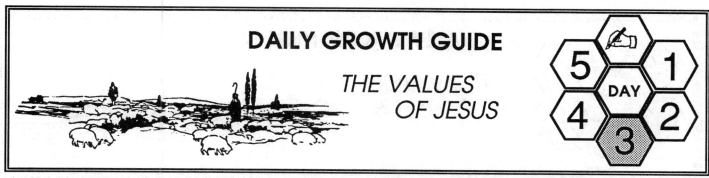

DAY THREE: THE VALUES OF JESUS: RIGHT TO HAPPINESS
SCRIPTURE READING PHILIPPIANS 2:3-8

"I have a right to happiness!"
Really? Do you also have a right to live in a palace, or never get the flu?
Is the "pursuit of happiness" the most important value in life?
How did Jesus value it?

1. In verses 3 and 4, what viewpoint is taken toward a "right to happiness?"

2. In verse 6, what "rights" could Jesus have exercised?

3. In verse 7, what did He deliberately choose to do with them?

4. In verse 8, what was His motive for doing so?

5. What does this teach us about exercising a "right to happiness?"

THOUGHT FOR THE DAY:
*FOR JESUS, A "RIGHT TO HAPPINESS" DIDN'T MAKE MUCH SENSE. FAR
MORE IMPORTANT TO OUR LORD WAS BECOMING A BONDSERVANT,
REDEEMING MEN BY HIS DEATH ON A CROSS. HOW MANY MEN CAN
YOU COUNT ON WHO ARE WORLD FAMOUS BECAUSE THEY CHOSE
TO BE HAPPY? HAPPINESS IS A BYPRODUCT, NOT A RIGHT!*

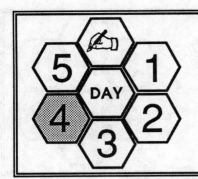

DAILY GROWTH GUIDE

THE VALUES OF JESUS

DAY FOUR: THE VALUE OF JESUS: LIFE

SCRIPTURE READING: JOHN 11:25-26

1. **How would Jesus have defined** *"life,"* **according to these verses?**

   ☐ "Animated existence," or "active vitality"

   ☐ The period from birth to death

   ☐ A person's manner of living

   ☐ "I am the Life"

2. **In what way is Jesus "Life," and "Life" is Jesus?**
   (Check all answers you consider valid:)

   ☐ True existence requires my receiving Him into my being.

   ☐ Life doesn't depend on outside circumstances, but a relationship with Him.

   ☐ The teachings of Jesus help me enjoy living.

3. **What new light does this verse shed on Paul's comments that** *"Christ lives in me"* **- and,** *"Christ in you, the hope of glory?"*

THOUGHT FOR THE DAY:
"ALL WHO HAVE NOT RUN AWAY FROM DEATH BUT HAVE STARED IT IN THE FACE, WHO KNOW LIFE THROUGH CHRIST AND HAVE HONESTLY SEARCHED OUT THE MEANING OF THIS EARTHLY EXISTENCE, CAN LIVE ABOVE FEAR."
...H. S. Vigeveno

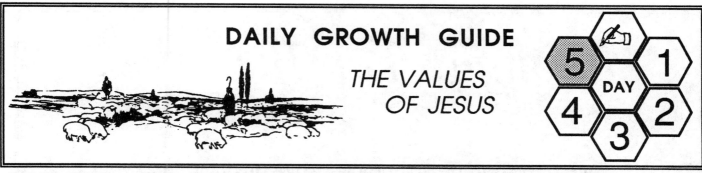

DAILY GROWTH GUIDE

THE VALUES OF JESUS

DAY FIVE: THE VALUES OF JESUS: ADAM'S CHILDREN

SCRIPTURE READING: MATTHEW 9:36-38

1. What two characteristics of Adam's children upset Jesus?

2. Realizing that sheep have utterly no sense of direction, why do you think they displayed those characteristics?

3. Why do you think Jesus switched from describing Adam's children as "sheep" to a "harvest field" in this passage?

   ☐ There is no significance in the switch

   ☐ His reasons for doing so are not understandable

   ☐ "Sheep" reveal lostness; "grain" reveals ease of ingathering

   ☐ Farmers would appreciate His allusions to their work

4. Why do we not share Jesus' feeling that Adam's children are reachable?

THOUGHT FOR THE DAY:
REACHING ONE PERSON AT A TIME IS THE BEST WAY OF REACHING THE WORLD IN TIME.

Thought For The Week

"To love at all is to be vulnerable. Love anything, and your heart will certainly be wrung and possibly be broken. If you want to make sure of keeping it intact, you must give your heart to no one. Wrap it carefully round with hobbies and little luxuries; avoid all entanglements; lock it up safe in the casket or coffin of your selfishness. And in that casket of selfishness your heart begins to change. It becomes hard, unbreakable, unredeemable. The only place outside Heaven where you can be perfectly safe from all dangers of love is Hell."

C. S. Lewis, "The Four Loves"

Be imitators of God, therefore, as dearly loved children and live a life of love, just as Christ loved us and gave Himself up for us as a fragrant offering and sacrifice to God.

• Ephesians 5:1

7

THE MAKING OF
A SERVANT:
MOSES, THE
"SOMEBODY"

PERSONAL INVENTORY

Just before watching the videotape, thoughtfully answer these questions...

	AGREE	UNCERTAIN	DISAGREE
The Lord helps those who help themselves	☐	☐	☐
Only the secure can serve others	☐	☐	☐
My conduct is strongly guided by the approval or disapproval of my friends	☐	☐	☐
At a party, I bend my values to fit the "climate" of the group around me	☐	☐	☐
It's impossible to take Christian values into my everyday world; they are impractical	☐	☐	☐
Influencing people is very important to me	☐	☐	☐
I would quit my job rather than compromise a principle God has given to me as a Christian	☐	☐	☐
I often worry about my future	☐	☐	☐
I believe in taking care of my own needs first, and helping others second	☐	☐	☐
I have never been able to totally rely on God to provide what I need in life	☐	☐	☐

VIDEO PRESENTATION

Divide the Outline among the group members to review after video is viewed.

THE MAKING OF A SERVANT: MOSES THE "SOMEBODY"

1. **REVIEW OF LIFE PRINCIPLES**
   A. Truths we have learned before:
      1. Our significance is in who we are, not what we do
      2. What we do is because of what we are
      3. As servants, we are doing what God is doing
   B. Ephesians 1:10 tells us what He is doing

2. **SERVING: OUR ONLY WAY TO SHARE GOD'S LOVE**
   A. Reasons why this is true:
      1. Serving reveals our security as God's children
      2. We give to those who cannot give in return
   B. The secular world expects this of us
      1. They resent us when we do not serve
      2. God's "free enterprise system" is unique
   C. Illustration: Pastor and Gangster

3. **MOSES: A "SOMEBODY" ENROUTE TO "SERVANTHOOD"**
   A. His many qualities described
      1. His coming predicted to Abraham
      2. Glowingly described in Acts 7
      3. At age 40, a real "Somebody!"
   B. He kills an Egyptian
      1. Loses everything...Flees to desert
      2. What caused him to be a failure?

4. **THE SUPPOSITION OF A SOMEBODY**
   A. He was keenly concerned about what men thought
   B. Yet, he never looked UP to get God's thoughts
   C. He had totally lost his sense of God's presence
   D. He was not committed to God's plan
   E. Peter: another example of a "Somebody"

5. **PRINCIPLES OF SERVANTHOOD**
   A. Thaligam: example of obedience
   B. Wahab: example of dependence

6. **THE MOTTO OF A TRUE SERVANT**
   (See last page in this unit)

DISCUSSION TOPICS

*Always begin with your DAILY REPORT TIME
Let each person share briefly;
report insights gained by completing
the Practical Assignment.*

DAILY REPORT TIME: (10 minutes) Let each person share for no more than 1 minute, reporting insights gained from the Weekly Assignment. Then use the remaining portion of the 10 minutes for a general discussion of your findings.

SMALL GROUP ACTIVITY: (20 minutes)

Each person role plays a character listed below. The person in each group wearing the newest pair of shoes takes the first name; the rest are distributed clockwise.

(1) JOHN THE BAPTIST

(2) MOSES, THE "SOMEBODY"

(3) DORCAS (ACTS 9:36-40)

(4) SAUL OF TARSUS

(5) MATTHEW, AN UNCONVERTED TAX COLLECTOR

You are asked to act out the characteristics of the person assigned to you. For five minutes, you will stand and briefly visit with the others in the room, who will also be acting out roles. At the end of the five minutes, return to your group and discuss:

1. WHAT CONTRAST DID YOU SEE BETWEEN THE SERVANT AND NON-SERVANT TYPES?

2. HOW DID THE NON-SERVANTS DEMONSTRATE THE "SUPPOSITION OF A SOMEBODY?"

This is your PRACTICAL ASSIGNMENT for this coming week...

RETURN TO YOUR PERSONAL EVALUATION TIME, USING THE QUESTIONS ON THE WEEKLY REPORT SHEET. EXPAND THE DECISIONS YOU MADE LAST WEEK TO INCLUDE THOSE OFFERED FOR YOUR CONSIDERATION THIS WEEK.

You probably think of the items you listed last week in terms of the future. Perhaps you think you will do them "someday," when conditions are right. However, these are matters which are important to your development *now!* The very fact that you listed them indicates God has spoken to you in a significant way.

They will serve as valuable sources of information to help you move into a new lifestyle. Your further personal spiritual growth depends upon your actualizing these "theoretical" conditions. Could you try one of these items this week? It is important to act on certain feelings to discover what would happen if we put them into practice.

If the conditions are not right to fully test one of your decisions, is there a way you could act out the spirit of it? For example, if someone desired to help hurting persons by establishing a group for them, would it be possible this week just to spend time with one such person?

Try a test...you'll be surprised at the results!

PRACTICAL ASSIGNMENT

REVIEW THE TWELVE THINGS YOU WROTE DOWN ON LAST WEEK'S REPORT SHEET. SELECT FROM THEM ONE THING YOU CAN BEGIN TO ACTUALIZE THIS WEEK. WRITE IT IN THE BOX:

1. I chose this first because:

2. I can take this "first step" this week to actualize this vision:

**REMEMBER: HAPPY ARE THEY WHO DREAM DREAMS....
...AND ARE WILLING TO PAY THE PRICE TO MAKE THEM COME TRUE!**

Name
_____

DAILY GROWTH GUIDE

ACTUALIZING YOUR DREAMS

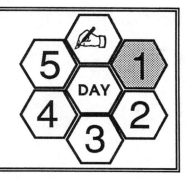

DAY ONE: LIFE....ABUNDANTLY!
SCRIPTURE READING: JOHN 10:10

1. Your WEEKLY ASSIGNMENT challenges you to "actualize" (to make real, to create what has been a dream) one of the goals you wrote down last week. As you meditate on this verse, what does God say to you about making that goal real? Meditate on this for several minutes...and then use this page to write your feelings. Later on, they will be meaningful to you!

   (In other words, read this verse in the "Listening Room!")

THOUGHT FOR THE DAY:
"IT IS HARD TO SEE HOW A GREAT MAN CAN BE AN ATHEIST. DOUBTERS DO NOT ACHIEVE. SKEPTICS DO NOT CONTRIBUTE. CYNICS DO NOT CREATE. FAITH IS THE GREAT MOTIVE POWER AND NO MAN REALIZES HIS FULL POSSIBILITIES UNLESS HE HAS THE DEEP CONVICTION THAT LIFE IS ETERNALLY IMPORTANT AND THAT HIS WORK, WELL DONE, IS A PART OF AN UNENDING PLAN."
...Calvin Coolidge

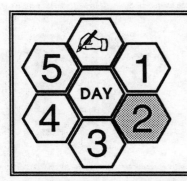

DAILY GROWTH GUIDE

ACTUALIZING YOUR DREAMS

DAY TWO: WORKING HIS WORKS
SCRIPTURE READING: JOHN 9:4

1. In this verse, what causes you to feel an urgency about actualizing the "dreams" you have written down?

2. Why has it been impossible in the past to actualize the specific dream which you have selected to begin this week?

3. What makes it different now?

THOUGHT FOR THE DAY:
SAMUEL JOHNSON WROTE TODAY'S VERSE IN GREEK ACROSS THE FACE OF HIS WATCH WHEN HE BEGAN WORK ON THE FIRST DICTIONARY OF THE ENGLISH LANGUAGE. HE THEN PRAYED: "OH, GOD, WHO HAS HITHERTO SUPPORTED ME, ENABLE ME TO PROCEED IN THIS LABOUR--THAT WHEN I SHALL RENDER UP, AT THE LAST DAY, AN ACCOUNT OF THE TALENT COMMITTED TO ME, I MAY RECEIVE PARDON, FOR THE SAKE OF JESUS CHRIST. AMEN."

DAILY GROWTH GUIDE

ACTUALIZING YOUR DREAMS

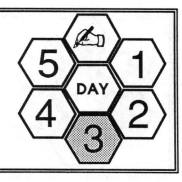

DAY THREE: WHAT DO YOU SEE?
SCRIPTURE READING: GENESIS 13:15-18

1. In what sense was Abram in the "LISTENING ROOM" in this passage?

☐ He had told God what he wanted, and God was about to give it to him

☐ He felt God ought to give him a big reward because of his generosity to Lot

☐ He had no idea what God was going to say to him

2. Do you think Abram could have had this land in any other way? Explain your answer:

3. Why do you think God told Abram what He would do in the future?

4. What difference did it make in Abram's life to be able to actualize this promise given him by God?

THOUGHT FOR THE DAY:
FAITH IS BELIEVING THAT SOMETHING IS SO WHEN IT IS NOT SO,
BECAUSE YOU KNOW YOUR GOD IS GOING TO MAKE IT SO!

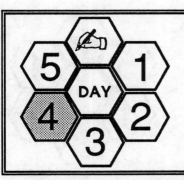

DAILY GROWTH GUIDE

ACTUALIZING YOUR DREAMS

DAY FOUR: BELIEVING IN THE LORD
SCRIPTURE READING: GENESIS 15:1-6

1. **Once again, Abram is in the "Listening Room!" What does God say?**

2. **How does this promise of the future differ from yesterday's verse?**

3. **Abram could now actualize his dream! He knew what God would do. What difference does it make to us for God to shape our dreams?**

4. **Could Abram ever have come up with such a "goal" for himself, if left alone and without God? What about you? Is your goal given by God?**

THOUGHT FOR THE DAY:
WHEN GOD HAS A GIGANTIC TASK TO BE PERFORMED, FAITH GETS THE CONTRACT!

DAILY GROWTH GUIDE

ACTUALIZING YOUR DREAMS

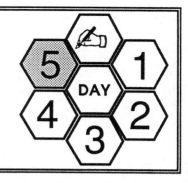

DAY FIVE: IT'S ALL IN WHAT YOU SEE!
SCRIPTURE READING: NUMBERS 13:31, 14:6-9

1. What did this first set of spies see when they scouted the land?

2. What did Joshua and Caleb see, as they scouted the same land?

3. What caused the two groups to "see" differently?

4. Which group do you identify with most closely? Why?

THOUGHT FOR THE DAY:
YOU DO NOT TEST THE RESOURCES OF GOD UNTIL YOU TRY THE IMPOSSIBLE.

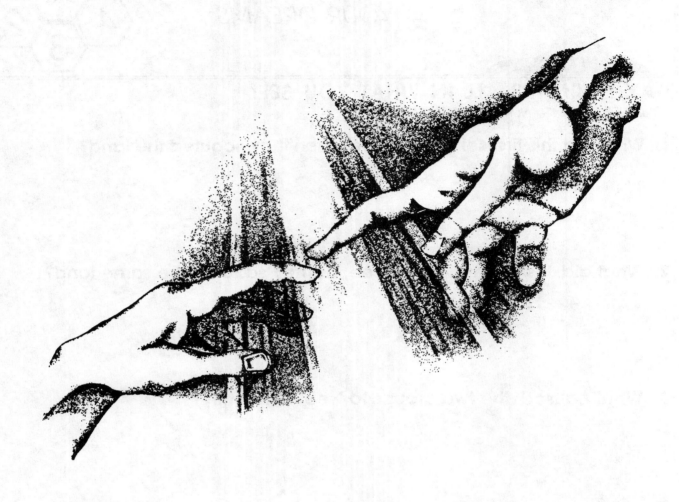

THE MOTTO OF A TRUE SERVANT

1. It is my business to do the will of God.
2. It is God's business to take care of me.
3. Therefore, I don't ever have to be afraid of anything!

8

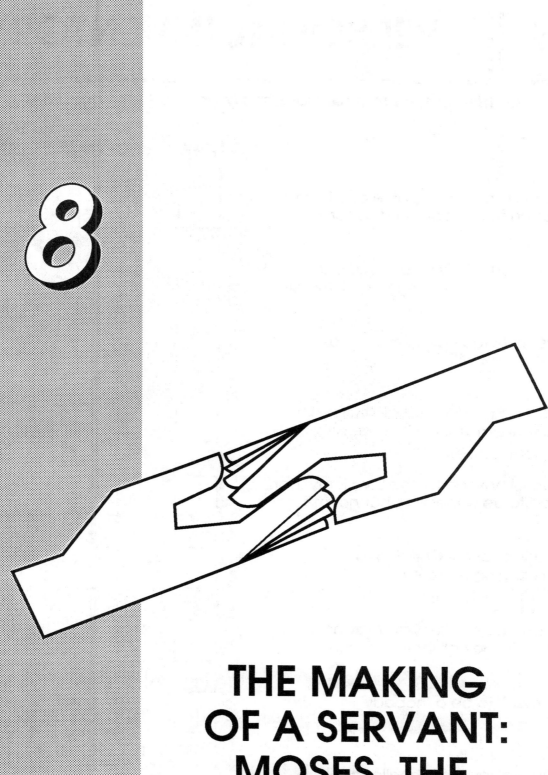

THE MAKING
OF A SERVANT:
MOSES, THE
"NOBODY"

PERSONAL INVENTORY

Just before watching the videotape, thoughtfully answer these questions...

	AGREE	UNCERTAIN	DISAGREE
I do not consider myself capable of bringing another person to accept Christ as Lord.	☐	☐	☐
I prefer to support others who can reach unbelievers, rather than trying to do it myself	☐	☐	☐
I have never felt God calling me to do anything particular with my life	☐	☐	☐
I consider myself to be untrained in the skills needed to share my faith with others	☐	☐	☐
I feel the work I now do for the Lord is my "part"... Others need to be witnessing, but *not me*	☐	☐	☐
It is necessary for every Christian to be involved in bringing unbelievers to salvation	☐	☐	☐
Someone lives in my *oikos* who may never accept Christ if I do not share my faith	☐	☐	☐
I consider myself to be a "nobody"	☐	☐	☐
When risk is involved, I am challenged!	☐	☐	☐
Our church spends too much time inside the building, and not enough time reaching unbelievers	☐	☐	☐

VIDEO PRESENTATION

Divide the Outline among the group members to review after video is viewed.

THE MAKING OF A SERVANT: MOSES, THE "NOBODY"

1. MOSES FAILS AS A "SOMEBODY"
   A. He tried to do the WORK of God
       1. He did not enter the "Listening Room"
       2. He listened, instead, to his friends
       3. His life collapsed
   B. He had lost his sense of God's presence
       1. When this happens, we come to a fork in the road
       2. The choice: be a SERVANT, or a NOBODY!

2. MOSES BECAME A "NOBODY"
   A. He tended sheep
       1. Convinced he was a failure
       2. Relieved to be free of responsibility
   B. We have a tendency to do the same:
       1. Our spirit is broken
       2. We feel we are "different"
   C. We think we have a "right" to be a NOBODY

3. THE CRISIS WE FACE
   A. Population Explosion
       1. Two billion in 1930
       2. Four billion in 1974
       3. Six billion by 2000!
   B. Christianity in trouble...
       1. Now: 44 christians to win one convert
       2. Needed: 4 converts for ONE Christian

4. THE ATTITUDE OF A NOBODY
   A. I can't do it; why try?
   B. I will support those who "can"
   C. Unfortunately, no one else "can!"
   D. Pastor is often the only one reaching anyone
   E. Illustration: automobile dealership, run like a church, would go bankrupt!

5. THE DANGER OF "BEING DISCIPLED"
   A. *Another* long process, keeping us from whitened fields
   B. A good thing, but not an end in itself
       1. We must eliminate all the "NOBODY" excuses
       2. The fields *are* white, waiting for us to come!

DISCUSSION TOPICS

Always begin with your DAILY REPORT TIME
Let each person share briefly;
report insights gained by completing
the Practical Assignment.

DAILY REPORT TIME: (10 minutes) Let each person share for no more than 1 minute, reporting insights gained from the Weekly Assignment. Then use the remaining portion of the 10 minutes for a general discussion of your findings.

DISCUSSION QUESTIONS: (25 minutes)
Read Exodus 2:15-25 aloud

1. What kinds of activities occupied the life of Moses in these verses? Were any of his activities wrong, or evil? How do his activities parallel our own?

2. While Moses was living his own lifestyle, what was happening to the Israelites? Did Moses feel any deep concern for them? How would you feel if you had been Moses?

3. Was Moses in any way responsible for the plight of the Israelites by withdrawing for 40 years in the desert, when he knew his life's work was to set them free? Do we have any responsibility for those who are in "bondage" around *us?*

4. What can be done to stop the loss of Christian expansion as the population explodes? *What part of the answer should I assume as my task?*

WHAT WILL BE THE FUTURE OF YOUR FRIENDS AND RELATIVES?

Think about that this week. As you review the people in your life...your friends, contacts, and relatives...ask yourself, "Where will this person's lifestyle take them to in five years? In fifty years? In eternity?"

As you think about them, as you observe them, consider the possibility of someone intercepting them with a servant heart. (Apart from *you*, that is!) *Is it likely to happen?*

What responsibility do you feel toward them? Is the situation parallel to Moses, who lived an easy life in the desert while Israel writhed in bondage? Is there a mission you have to those around you?

Just....*observe!* That's all your assignment calls for you to do. Of course, if you become caught up by the need to share your faith, to serve these persons, it would be most pleasing to the Lord if you were to do so!

PRACTICAL ASSIGNMENT

FROM YOUR OBSERVATIONS, LIST THE NAMES OF THOSE AMONG YOUR FRIENDS AND RELATIVES WHO ARE NOT YET BELIEVERS:

WHAT DO YOU CONSIDER THEIR FUTURES TO BE....IF THEY DO NOT BECOME CHRISTIANS?

A. In five years?

B. In fifty years?

C. In eternity?

Name _____

DAILY GROWTH GUIDE

THE CALL OF MOSES

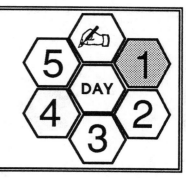

DAY ONE: THE BURNING BUSH
SCRIPTURE READING: EXODUS 3:1-10

1. What is the significance of God appearing to Moses in a burning bush?
- ☐ Fire purifies all it touches
- ☐ God had to do something to get his attention

2. Why did Moses have to remove his shoes?
- ☐ He was to feel relaxed and at ease before Jehovah
- ☐ The ground before God was holy

3. In verse 8, who is described as delivering the Israelites?
- ☐ God
- ☐ Moses

4. How do we know God was aware of the suffering of Israel? (v.9)

5. Why does verse 10 require a Master-Servant relationship?
- ☐ God is making the decisions
- ☐ Moses is recommending a solution to God

THOUGHT FOR THE DAY:
THERE IS AN AWESOME UNIQUENESS ABOUT MEETINGS BETWEEN GOD AND MAN. TO MOSES, HE CAME IN A BURNING BUSH; TO PAUL, AS A BRIGHT LIGHT; TO ANOTHER, AS A STILL, SMALL VOICE. HAVE YOU MET HIM? IF SO, THE DETAILS ARE NOT NEARLY AS SIGNIFICANT AS THE ASSIGNMENT!

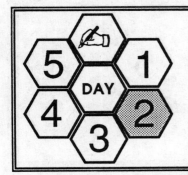

DAILY GROWTH GUIDE

THE CALL OF MOSES

DAY TWO: A "NOBODY" BEGINS TO SQUIRM
SCRIPTURE READING: EXODUS 3:11-12

1. What was the excuse Moses used to avoid serving God? (v.11)

☐ "I have signed a contract to tend sheep."

☐ "I am a NOBODY. I failed in the past."

2. In verse 12, what solution did God give to eliminate Moses' excuse?

3. Why do you think we always look first at our own inadequacies?

☐ We are used to getting our significance from what we do

☐ We are not used to trusting God's power over our own abilities

☐ Neither of the above is correct

☐ Both of the above are correct

THOUGHT FOR THE DAY:
NOBODIES DON'T GIVE UP BEING NOBODIES WITHOUT A FIGHT!

DAILY GROWTH GUIDE

*THE CALL
OF MOSES*

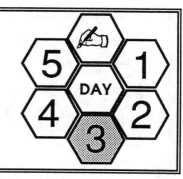

DAY THREE: ANOTHER LAME EXCUSE!
SCRIPTURE READING: EXODUS 3:13-22

1. **What is the next excuse Moses the "Nobody" uses with God? (verse 13)**

2. **What is the equivalent excuse used by "nobodies" today?**

    ☐ "I have a job in the church already"

    ☐ "I tithe; let someone else do that job"

    ☐ "I don't have enough knowledge about God; I need more training"

    ☐ "Perhaps in the *future* I'll be ready---"

    (NOTE: God's answer to Moses includes His revealing of His personal name: *"Jehovah. "*It means,
    "I shall be all that is necessary as each occasion arises." Armed with His name alone, Moses knew
    more about Him than anyone in Egypt!)

3. **Read thoughtfully the long, long answer God provides to Moses.
    Why do you think God went into such detail?**

    ☐ Moses would know exactly what to expect as events unfolded

    ☐ Moses would not have to bother God for further directions

4. **How does God's explanation relate to the meaning of *"Jehovah?"***

*THOUGHT FOR THE DAY:
GOD'S DIVINE PURPOSE FOR US MAY BRING A THRILL; HIS DIVINE
PLAN FOR FULFILLING THAT PURPOSE MAY BRING A CHILL! ONCE
COMMITTED TO SERVANTHOOD, ONE MUST NOT GROW FAINT
HEARTED. WHAT GOD BEGINS, HE COMPLETES.*

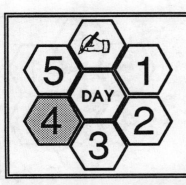 

DAILY GROWTH GUIDE

THE CALL OF MOSES

DAY FOUR: A THIRD EXCUSE
SCRIPTURE READING: EXODUS 4: 1-9

1. **What excuse does Moses try to use next?**

2. **How does the use of the rod prove God's power is with Moses?**

3. **Why can we expect God to provide such power today to His servants?**

4. **What example of God's power have you seen or experienced?**

THOUGHT FOR THE DAY:
THOSE WHO RECEIVE GOD'S WILL MAY EXPECT TO RECEIVE HIS POWER TO PERFORM IT. BUT, SUCH POWER BECOMES AVAILABLE AT THE POINT OF NEED, NOT AT THE RECEIVING OF HIS WILL. POWER IS PROVIDED WHEN IT IS NEEDED, NOT IN ADVANCE. MANY OF US NEVER DISCOVER GOD'S POWER BECAUSE WE NEVER ADVANCE TO THE NEED FOR IT.

DAY FIVE; WOULD YOU BELIEVE ...A FOURTH EXCUSE?

SCRIPTURE READING: EXODUS 4:10-12; ACTS 7:22

1. What is the fourth excuse Moses, the "Nobody," uses with God?

2. Why do you think he is still trying to excuse himself?

3. Do we do much the same thing? If so, why?

4. In verse 11, how does God reveal His growing indignation with Moses?

5. How does Acts 7:22 reveal the lameness of Moses' excuse?

6. If you had been God, what would you have done at this point about Moses?

THOUGHT FOR THE DAY:
WE INSULT GOD WHEN WE TELL HIM WE ARE INADEQUATE. IT IS THE SAME AS ACCUSING HIM OF BOTCHING HIS CREATION WHEN HE MADE US. THE ONLY WAY A "NOBODY" COULD EXIST WOULD BE FOR GOD TO MAKE A PERSON THAT WAY. AS THE COUNTRY PREACHER SAID, "GOD DON'T SPONSOR NO FLOPS!"

Thought For The Week

This is a critical week for you as you take LIFE BASIC TRAINING. Records reveal that it is during this week that most of the dropouts from the class take place. Interviews with those who have done so indicate why...

The inevitable direction of the material is now understood. The choice is here! "Will I become a Servant of God, or will I not?" Like the Rich Young Ruler, some who stand where you are today have turned away, feeling the cost was too great!

We tend to back away from Servanthood for the same reason Peter didn't want Jesus washing his feet at the last supper. We know that if He washed feet, then we will have to do so also...and we have no intention of doing so!

If you are really struggling with the Servanthood decision, you owe it to yourself to finish the final three sessions. That poor Young Ruler! He knew what he walked away WITH...his old riches intact. What he did not know, and what he would NEVER know, was what "might have been" if he had obeyed Jesus. Imagine the potential "wealth that is real" he forfeited by his decision.

If you get this far on your journey and turn back, WILL THERE EVER BE ANOTHER OCCASION IN YOUR LIFE WHEN YOU WILL COME THIS FAR AGAIN? Think about it. It's your life. Will it be "abundant," or will it never, ever be any more than it has been in the past? Are you REALLY willing to settle for that?

By faith Moses, when he had grown up, refused to be known as the son of Pharaoh's daughter. He chose to be mistreated along with the people of God rather than to enjoy the pleasures of sin for a short time. He regarded disgrace for the sake of Christ as of greater value than the treasures of Egypt, because he was looking ahead to his reward.
• Hebrews 11:25-26

9

MOSES' REJECTION
OF GOD'S
COMMISSION

PERSONAL INVENTORY

Just before watching the videotape, thoughtfully answer these questions...

	AGREE	UNCERTAIN	DISAGREE
A past failure makes it hard for me to face new situations where I might fail once again	☐	☐	☐
I don't feel I have enough knowledge about God to represent Him before Adam's children	☐	☐	☐
I'll do nearly anything to keep from feeling rejection from another person	☐	☐	☐
Success is very important to me	☐	☐	☐
I would move to another job or city if the Lord directed me to do so	☐	☐	☐
I do not worry much about the purpose for which I exist	☐	☐	☐
I have never really felt responsible for bringing others to know Christ as Lord	☐	☐	☐
I feel that I am an acceptable person	☐	☐	☐
I enjoy church activities, but avoid involvement in all church visitation activities	☐	☐	☐
I have a strong conviction that my life is meant to be used by God to reach unbelievers	☐	☐	☐

VIDEO PRESENTATION

Divide the Outline among the group members to review after video is viewed.

MOSES' REJECTION OF GOD'S COMMISSION

1. **MOSES' STRONG RESISTANCE TO GOD'S CALL**
   A. Daily growth guide showed 4 excuses
      1. Always a struggle to enter servanthood
      2. Reason: still struggling for personal significance
      3. Moses has "tuned in, turned on, dropped out"
   B. Four excuses...but only 2 reasons:
      1. Fear of failure
      2. Fear of success

2. **MOSES' INDIFFERENCE TO THE SUFFERING SLAVES**
   A. Tended sheep while Israel suffered
      1. Lived without concern for them
      2. God's children today doing the same thing
   B. Desperate plight of today's world....
      1. Moses' indifference caused 2 million to suffer
      2. Our indifference related to 2 BILLION

3. **THE ATTITUDE OF MOSES AS HE FACED GOD**
   A. He made four excuses
      1. We make excuses, too: age, education, shyness, etc.
      2. All are a protective shield for selfishness
   B. Moses' alternatives:
      1. Jethro would leave him the farm
      2. An easy life ahead

4. **GOD DEALT WITH MOSES**
   A. Moses had no "Listening Room" in his life
   B. God said *"YOU, YOU, YOU!"*
   C. His obedience was finally brought about by God's insistence

5. **WHAT WAS GOD'S CALL TO MOSES?**
   A. Not a call to a TASK
   B. Rather, a call to be a SERVANT

6. **ILLUSTRATION: CHINESE GIRL IN SINGAPORE**

DISCUSSION TOPICS

Always begin with your DAILY REPORT TIME
Let each person share briefly;
report insights gained by completing
the Practical Assignment.

WEEKLY REPORT TIME: (10 minutes) Let each person share for no more than 1 minute, reporting insights gained from the weekly assignment. Then use the remaining portion of the 10 minutes for a general discussion of your findings.

COMPLETE THE FOLLOWING TWO SENTENCES:

During the videotape today, I found myself giving a great deal of thought to...

I identify closely with Moses in the following ways...

DISCUSSION:

1. Share your responses to the sentences above, dealing with one at a time. (10 minutes)

2. Discuss this comment from the videotape:

> "Nobodies" do not see themselves as they really are, because they sift everything through a screen of self-doubt.

Do you agree, or disagree? What spiritual problem is faced by such a person? What solution is there to this spiritual problem?

This is your PRACTICAL ASSIGNMENT for this coming week...

EXPERIENCE THE "LISTENING ROOM" THIS WEEK. FOLLOW THE DIRECTIONS BELOW. SEEK THE DIRECTIONS OF THE MASTER TO YOU, THE SERVANT. DO AS HE INSTRUCTS! FOR THAT, THERE IS NO REPORT....JUST OBEDIENCE.

YOU ARE INVITED TO MEET WITH.....JEHOVAH GOD!

Learn how to use the "Listening Room" we have been talking about, if you have not done so already. Follow these steps:

SELECT A SPECIAL PRIVATE AREA FOR YOUR "LISTENING ROOM."

One couple selected an infrequently used room in their home. A Bible was placed in it for reading. They made a simple Cross out of two small branches, which they leaned against a wall. With thumb tacks, they placed slips of paper on this cross. Each slip contained their needs, concerns, or names of people they were praying for. It was their way of "taking to the cross" the details of life. Soon, the room became precious to them. From that cross they found many, many answers to their prayers.

SELECT A SPECIAL TIME TO BE IN THE "LISTENING ROOM."

For many, it will be early in the morning. Return to it as often as you desire, but always have a *specific* time to be in the "Listening Room." Remember...when you enter it, have a "sense of God" in that place. Of course, He is with you *everywhere* you go, but there is something important about your deliberately being with Him.

TAKE AN OPEN HEART, AN OPEN MIND TO THAT ROOM.

Don't go to *ask;* go to *listen.* Read His scripture with a listening spirit. It will not be long before He will begin to "speak" to you about your ministry of servanthood.

OBEY THE MASTER'S ORDERS.

Some of them may surprise you! If you have a hungry, open heart, you will find Him prepared to use you in greater ways than you ever dreamed possible. When He places that "impossible" assignment before you, respond by faith. You'll find a whole new way of living as a result!

PRACTICAL ASSIGNMENT

DESCRIBE YOUR "LISTENING ROOM": WHERE IS IT LOCATED, ETC.?

WHAT TIME HAVE YOU RESERVED TO BE IN IT?

WHAT HAS GOD SAID TO YOU IN THAT ROOM?

WHAT ORDERS HAS HE GIVEN YOU IN THAT ROOM?

Name _____

DAILY GROWTH GUIDE

COMPLETE YOUR COMMITMENT

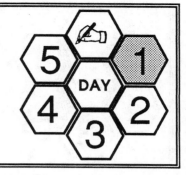

DAY ONE: GOOD SOIL
SCRIPTURE READING: LUKE 8:15

1. **What three characteristics of the seed in good soil are mentioned?**

    1.

    2.

    3.

2. **Why do these characteristics help the seed to grow?**

3. **Why is commitment (perseverance) necessary to yield a "harvest?"**

4. **How long did Moses' commitment to deliver Israel continue?**

    ☐ Until he tired of it

    ☐ Until he finally died

5. **What is your "track record" on following through on commitments?**

THOUGHT FOR THE DAY:
GIVE YOUR COMMITMENT TO SERVANTHOOD TIME TO BEAR FRUIT!
USUALLY OUR FAILURES ARE THE RESULT OF QUITTING HALF WAY
THROUGH.

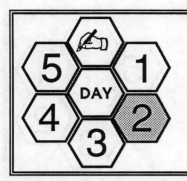

DAILY GROWTH GUIDE

COMPLETE
YOUR COMMITMENT

DAY TWO: GOOD HUSBANDRY
SCRIPTURE READING: PHILIPPIANS 1:6

1. **Who is the one who starts the good work in you?**

2. **How long will He remain committed to doing what he started?**

3. **How long will it take for the task to be completed?**
   - ☐ Five years
   - ☐ Ten years
   - ☐ Not until Christ returns again

4. **How long did it take Christ to finish His mission on earth?**
   - ☐ Thirty three years
   - ☐ His entire life span, until death came

5. **How long will the Father "cultivate " your growth?**
   - ☐ Until He gets tired of your slowness to bear fruit
   - ☐ Until you become fruitful
   - ☐ Until you are taken home to be with Him

6. **What did it cost our Lord to make such a commitment to you?**

THOUGHT FOR THE DAY:
YOU DON'T STOP IN YOUR COMMITMENT TO SERVANTHOOD SIMPLY BECAUSE YOU FEEL HURT OR PAIN. IT'S REQUIRED FOR EVERY WORTHWHILE COMMITMENT, INCLUDING GIVING BIRTH TO A CHILD.

DAILY GROWTH GUIDE
COMPLETE YOUR COMMITMENT

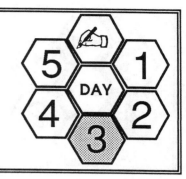

DAY THREE: GOOD CHOICES
SCRIPTURE READING: LUKE 4: 5-8

1. **What did Satan use to try to divert Jesus from His commitment?**

2. **For what price would you cancel your commitment of servanthood?**
   - [ ] For $75,000 in cash
   - [ ] To avoid a potential loss of $7,500
   - [ ] Both of the above
   - [ ] Neither of the above

3. **What is your "weakest point," known by Satan and used to tempt you?**

4. **What choice do you have when Satan tempts you?**
   - [ ] I can give in
   - [ ] I can flatly refuse him
   - [ ] I can consider whether it would harm anyone to yield

THOUGHT FOR THE DAY:
SATAN'S TRACK RECORD STRETCHES INTO HISTORY! HE HAS CONSTANTLY DANGLED A CARROT ON A STICK IN FRONT OF THOSE WHO HAVE CHOSEN THE COMMITTED PATH. WHENEVER HE CAN GET OUR EYES FOCUSED ON THE CARROT, WE FORGET OUR MISSION! WHAT CARROT DOES HE USE ON YOU?

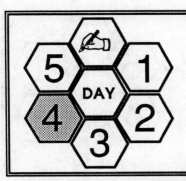

DAY FOUR: GOOD ATTITUDES
SCRIPTURE READING: PHILLIPIANS 4:11-13

1. **In your own words, describe the level of commitment Paul had:**

2. **What was his source of power? (Verse 13)**

3. **Which of the following were most important to his commitment?**

   ☐ Choosing to find God's resources in the "down" times

   ☐ Choosing to avoid the tough places

   ☐ Choosing to "tough it out" and wallow in self-pity

4. **How do you usually handle "downs?"**

   ☐ By finding Christ's strength and going on

   ☐ By terminating my commitment to servanthood

   ☐ By feeling I deserve better treatment by God

*THOUGHT FOR THE DAY:
EFFECTIVE SERVANTHOOD IS MORE ATTITUDE THAN APTITUDE!*

DAILY GROWTH GUIDE

COMPLETE YOUR COMMITMENT

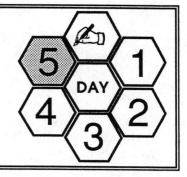

DAY FIVE: GOOD MODELS
SCRIPTURE READING: PHILIPPIANS 3:17

1. Why did Paul encourage them to use his life as a "model?"

☐ Because without "models" we find it hard to enter servanthood

☐ Because he wanted people to respect him and spread his fame

2. List below three names of servant "models" in your life:

1.

2.

3.

3. How do "models" help to raise our own threshold of commitment?

4. Who so "modeled" commitment to you that your threshold was raised?

5. Have you ever thanked that person for being a model to you?

THOUGHT FOR THE DAY:
*AN UNCOMMITTED LIFE IS A WORTHLESS LIFE. THERE IS NO EASY WAY
TO SAY IT; THERE IS NO USEFUL WAY TO LIVE IT, EITHER!*

Thought For The Week

Journeying to Tioman Island from Malaysia, we saw our first flying fish. Out of the water it came, skimming over the waves for 50 yards, and then disappearing into the sea again. How brief was its journey out of the brine!

Some of us relate to the Lord like flying fishes. We are totally submerged in a secular lifestyle all week long. We fill our minds with the refuse of our culture, watching endless television programs. We live in a world of business, education, medicine, etc., where four letter words are commonplace. Then, for a few brief hours (three?) on Sunday, we become flying fish. We sing, pray, think piously, and feel the exhilaration of being above the brine.

Then we return again to the old life style. Our habits are so deeply ingrained! We would no more think of missing our weekly flight out of the brine than we would think of *not* returning to the brine again! Both are habits, and as we all know, "habits" are always masters, and we are always their slaves.

When will being like "flying fish" end for us? We have become the recipients of *abundant life* - life in which every day is a special time to fly over the brine. Our King and Elder Brother, Jesus Christ, offers us the greater lifestyle: *SERVANTHOOD*. Do you want to fly? Are you ready?

...I consider my life worth nothing to me, if only I may finish the race and complete the task the Lord Jesus has given me--the task of testifying to the gospel of God's grace.

• Acts 20:24

10

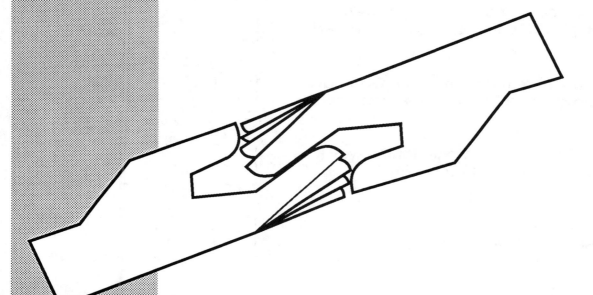

MOSES BECOMES THE SERVANT OF GOD

PERSONAL INVENTORY

Just before watching the videotape, thoughtfully answer these questions...

	AGREE	UNCERTAIN	DISAGREE
I consider being a true servant of God the highest honor I could ever know	☐	☐	☐
I am committed to pay any price necessary to do the work of my Master, Jesus Christ	☐	☐	☐
I have experienced moments when God's power was provided to me to do his assigned work	☐	☐	☐
I have known those moments when God gave me "marching orders," and I have responded obediently	☐	☐	☐
I often feel God "owes me one" for the way I have tried to live my life before Him	☐	☐	☐
I often trust myself instead of God	☐	☐	☐
I've made the ultimate commitment of a Christian: I have chosen to be His servant	☐	☐	☐
Listening to the Lord is a valuable part of my lifestyle these days	☐	☐	☐
God is going to use me more in the next twelve months than ever before in my life	☐	☐	☐
I make a decision and stick with it	☐	☐	☐

VIDEO PRESENTATION

Divide the Outline among the group members to review after video is viewed.

MOSES BECOMES THE SERVANT OF GOD

1. **THE ESTABLISHING OF THE RELATIONSHIP**
   A. By Exodus 14:31, a true relationship is established
      1. God's power did not come to Moses until he became a servant
      2. We also receive power only after we become a servant
   B. Moses forever after known as "The Servant of God"

2. **THE SERVANT WORD IS "OBEY"**
   A. The words "Succeed" and "Fail" are eliminated
      1. Being willing in advance to obey is crucial
      2. "No" and "Lord" do not fit each other
   B. Example: Luke 17:7-10
      1. There is no bonus for being obedient
      2. Expecting a reward for obedience is terrible egotism
   C. Once "significance" is solved, obedience is easy!

3. **GOD IS ADEQUATE FOR ALL OCCASIONS**
   A. Moses found His power ever present when needed
      1. Before Pharaoh, the Red Sea, etc.
      2. Better than a SELF MADE MAN is a GOD MADE MAN
   B. We ask Him to provide THINGS; He knows we need CONDITIONS
      1. These conditions make it possible for Him to provide what we really need
      2. If we don't face impossible problems, we'll never know His supply

4. **THE "SO SO PRINCIPLE"**
   A. Exodus 4:4, 6,7,19-20
   B. God says, "Do this..." - SO I do it!
   C. No possibility of saying "NO" when you are saying "SO"
   D. Usually our Master is "King Circumstance"
   E. When we say "SO," we are no longer controlled by circumstances

5. **THE GREATEST MAN IN HISTORY**
   A. Jesus! Philippians 2:7 tells us He was an OBEDIENT servant
   B. In verse 5: "Have this attitude in yourselves"

6. **WE ALL HAVE THE CAPACITY TO BECOME A SERVANT!**

DISCUSSION TOPICS

Always begin with your DAILY REPORT TIME
Let each person share briefly;
report insights gained by completing
the Practical Assignment.

WEEKLY REPORT TIME: (10 minutes) Let each person share for no more than 1 minute, reporting insights gained from the Weekly Assignment. Then use the remaining portion of the 10 minutes for a general discussion of your findings.

SERVANTHOOD ISSUES WORKSHEET (4 minutes)
(Rate yourself: "10" is high, "1" is low)

____ I invest most of my time satisfying my own needs

____ I doubt myself often, am shy and self-conscious

____ I seldom experiment with new ways of doing things

____ I resist the control of others: even God!

____ I take pride in my ability to overcome obstacles

____ I have strong ideals which affect everything I do

DISCUSSION QUESTIONS: (20 minutes)

1. How do the character traits above cause us to say "NO" or "SO?"

2. Which of them are good for a servant to have? Which are not?

3. What can be done to change our negative character traits?

4. Read Romans 12:1-2 aloud. Restate it all, saying the opposite. How do you feel about the restatement? Does it now describe a Christian?

> ### This is your PRACTICAL ASSIGNMENT for this coming week...
> OFFER TO SERVE YOUR PASTOR, ASSISTING HIM IN THE BUILDING OF THE NEXT LIFE BASIC TRAINING SEMINAR. ENLIST UP TO FIVE MEMBERS OF THE CHURCH TO ATTEND IT, SHARING WITH THEM WHAT LIFE BASIC TRAINING HAS MEANT TO YOU.

IT'S TIME TO SERVE!

In a few weeks, your Pastor will be forming another LIFE BASIC TRAINING class. When he does so, you are asked to serve him and your Lord by securing five members of the congregation to attend it. Your testimony about the value of the course is needed!

In this session, you should be given the names of persons you may contact. These are all members who have not taken the Seminar. During this week, contact them. Tell them what LIFE BASIC TRAINING has meant to you. Encourage them to attend the Seminar. Seek to get a tentative commitment from them at this time to attend.

Later, reconfirm their promise to attend. Your Pastor will work with you in preparation for the Seminar, and rely on you to serve the group during the Seminar. Your experience in your small group activities in LIFE BASIC TRAINING has been an excellent way to equip you for that ministry.

**MAY GOD BLESS YOU RICHLY
AS YOU LAUNCH OUT INTO OTHER TYPES OF MINISTRY!**

PRACTICAL ASSIGNMENT

DID YOU SECURE THE LIST OF PERSONS TO BE INVITED TO THE SEMINAR?

IN THE SPACES BELOW, LIST ALL THE NAMES AND THEIR RESPONSES TO YOUR INVITATION TO ATTEND. HAND THIS IN, SO YOUR PASTOR CAN REVIEW THE INFORMATION.

Name _____

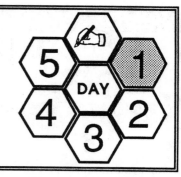
DAY ONE: THE POWERLESS RELIGIONISTS
SCRIPTURE READING: ACTS 3:1-3

1. **To what group did the lame man go for help? (verse 2)**
   - ☐ To the medical profession
   - ☐ To the bankers
   - ☐ To the people who went to worship God

2. **What did they give him? (verse 2)**
   - ☐ Tracts
   - ☐ Nothing
   - ☐ Alms (gold & silver)

3. **Did he expect anything else? If so, what?**

4. **If a lame man asked you for help, what would you give?**

THOUGHT FOR THE DAY:
THE PEOPLE WHO WERE GOING TO THE TEMPLE HAD NOTHING MORE
TO GIVE THE LAME MAN THAN THEIR GOLD. THEY GAVE THE BEST
THEY HAD TO GIVE...BUT IT DID NOT CHANGE THE MAN'S LAMENESS.
HE HAD BECOME CONTENT WITH GOLD. WHO COULD GIVE MORE?

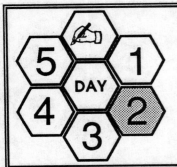

DAILY GROWTH GUIDE

WIRED FOR POWER

DAY TWO: MOSES EXPERIENCES GOD'S POWER
SCRIPTURE READING: EXODUS 4:1-7

1. What two evidences of God's power does Moses experience?

1.

2.

2. Apart from Moses and God, who observed this power?

3. Why did God expose Moses to His power here?

- ☐ Moses had never before experienced it
- ☐ He would not use what he had never experienced
- ☐ Both of the above
- ☐ Neither of the above

4. Why do Christians need a "burning bush" experience?

- ☐ Our power is limited by what we believe God can do
- ☐ We'll never expect more than we have experienced
- ☐ Both of the above
- ☐ Neither of the above

THOUGHT FOR THE DAY:
IN EIGHTY YEARS OF LIVING, MOSES HAD KNOWN NO POWER GREATER THAN HIS OWN STRENGTH. GOD KNEW HE COULD NOT FACE PHARAOH BEFORE PERSONALLY EXPERIENCING THE MIGHTY POWER OF THE MASTER. WHAT MANY OF US NEED IS A PERSONAL, FACE-TO-FACE ENCOUNTER WITH GOD'S POWER. IT'S TOUGH TO UNDERSTAND POWER YOU'VE NEVER EXPERIENCED!

DAILY GROWTH GUIDE

WIRED FOR POWER

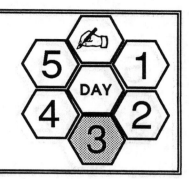

DAY THREE: PETER TOUCHES THE LAME MAN
SCRIPTURE READING: ACTS 3:3-8

1. What did the lame man expect from Peter and John?

2. Do you think he was disappointed when they said they had no gold?

3. What "TOUCH" point caused God's power to flow? (verse 7)

4. Did unbelief limit God's use of other worshipers to heal him?

5. Do you believe this actually happened?
   - ☐ Absolutely!
   - ☐ Unsure
   - ☐ Prefer to find a scientific explanation for it
   - ☐ Other

6. Does your own belief allow God to work through you?

THOUGHT FOR THE DAY:
IN NAZARETH, JESUS DID NO MIGHTY WORK "BECAUSE OF THEIR UNBELIEF." SOME CHURCHES REGULARLY SEE THE POWER OF GOD TOUCHING LIVES. OTHERS MECHANICALLY CONDUCT "PROGRAMS," AND NEVER KNOW THE SUPERNATURAL WORK OF GOD. WHY? IT'S A MATTER OF UNBELIEF, A MATTER OF WHAT WE EXPECT GOD TO DO.

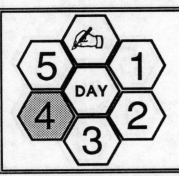

DAILY GROWTH GUIDE

WIRED FOR POWER

DAY FOUR: THE AMAZED TEMPLE WORSHIPERS
SCRIPTURE READING: ACTS 3:9-11; 4:4

1. **What were the two actions of the healed man? (verse 9)**
   1.

   2.

2. **Why were the temple goers so amazed?**
   ☐ They did not want men to be healed
   ☐ They had never previously observed such a healing

3. **What was the result of their seeing God's power? (4:4)**

4. **Does God reveal His power in such ways today?**

5. **In your opinion, why is His power limited today?**

THOUGHT FOR THE DAY:
IT IS TRUE THAT GOD DOES NOT THROW MIRACLES AROUND LIKE MILK BOTTLES. EACH ONE EVIDENCES HIS PRESENCE, HIS POWER. HOWEVER, THE LACK OF HIS POWER AMONG US IS THE RESULT OF UNBELIEF, NOTHING ELSE. HE IS THE SAME YESTERDAY, TODAY, AND FOREVER.

DAILY GROWTH GUIDE

WIRED FOR POWER

DAY FIVE: THE DANGER OF UNBELIEF
SCRIPTURE READING: MARK 9:17-24

1. In verse 18, who had been powerless to help this man?

2. In verse 22, what statement of doubt did the father make?

3. In verse 23, who did Jesus say limited His power?

4. In verse 24, what honest confession did the father make?

5. List any situations which may be limited by YOUR unbelief:

THOUGHT FOR THE DAY:
IS OUR PREOCCUPATION WITH CHURCH ACTIVITIES AN ESCAPE MECHANISM? IS IT A WAY TO AVOID FACING OUR POWERLESS CONDITION? IT'S HARD TO BE AROUND HURTING PERSONS WHEN YOU CANNOT HELP THEM! HOW MUCH OF OUR CHURCH WORK REQUIRES NO POWER AT ALL? SERVANTS DO MORE THAN RECEIVE THE MASTER'S PLANS: THEY ALSO RECEIVE HIS POWER!

Thought For The Week

The cylinder head is milled, or ground, as much as a twenty-thousandth of an inch to give a smaller cubic inch displacement in the cylinder head of the engine. This results in an increase in the compression ratio and a substantial increase in horsepower. To say it more simply, the greater the pressure, the greater the power.

This is also true in the spiritual realm. The greater the pressure upon us, the greater is our realization of our helplessness, with the result that our dependence upon God is greater and we receive spiritual power. Said Paul, "We were pressed out of measure, above strength," that is, human strength. When thus pressed, we press closer to the One whose "strength is made perfect in weakness," and who gives us "more grace."

> Pressed out of measure and pressed to all length,
> Pressed so intensely it seems beyond strength;
> Pressed in the body and pressed in the soul,
> Pressed in the mind till the dark surges roll;
> Pressure by foes, and pressure by friends,
> Pressure on pressure, till life nearly ends;
> Pressed into loving the staff and the rod,
> Pressed into knowing no helper but God;
> Pressed into liberty where nothing clings,
> Pressed into faith for impossible things;
> Pressed into living a life in the Lord,
> Pressed into living a Christ-life outpoured!
>
> -Walter B. Knight

"Do not fear what they fear; do not be frightened." But in your hearts set apart Christ as Lord. Always be prepared to give an answer to everyone who asks you to give the reason for the hope that you have.

• *I Peter 3:14-15*

11

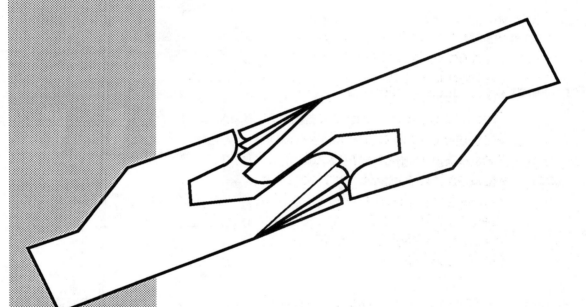

THE SEGULLAH
PEOPLE

PERSONAL INVENTORY

Just before watching the videotape, thoughtfully answer these questions...

	AGREE	UNCERTAIN	DISAGREE
I feel a need to be equipped to serve my Lord more completely	☐	☐	☐
I can see many coming to know the Lord through my servant life and ministry	☐	☐	☐
Pastors are "Ministers;" it's not possible for the rest to also be ministers	☐	☐	☐
I pray for friends who are unbelievers	☐	☐	☐
I consider myself a representative of Christ before unbelievers who are friends	☐	☐	☐
Whatever it would take to make Christ real to someone would be worth the cost	☐	☐	☐
I do not desire to minister to a group of atheistic, drug using young adults	☐	☐	☐
I usually "keep score" on the things I do for others in Christ's name	☐	☐	☐
I never think of myself as a "priest"	☐	☐	☐
I would like to continue what I have learned by taking additional training	☐	☐	☐

VIDEO PRESENTATION

Divide the Outline among the group members to review after video is viewed.

THE SEGULLAH PEOPLE

1. **TOUCH BASIC TRAINING: PREPARATION FOR SERVICE**
   A. Trains you as a part of a team
      1. You establish a SHARE GROUP
      2. You relate personally to your Pastor
      3. An "On-the-job" Seminary

2. **YOU ARE *"SEGULLAH"***
   A. *SEGULLAH* means *"special treasure"*
      1. King: rides through kingdom
      2. Selects finest gold, silver, precious stones
   B. "SO SO SERVANTS" are *SEGULLAH*
      1. There are Christians who are "Somebodies"
      2. And others who are "Nobodies"

3. ***"SEGULLAH"* SERVANTS ARE ALL PRIESTS**
   A. I Peter 2:5 and 9
      1. *"Holy"* Priesthood: because you are set apart for holy use
      2. *"Royal"* Priesthood: because you are a child of the King
   B. A Priest has two functions:
      1. Represents God before men
      2. Represents men before God

4. **WE ARE NEVER PRIESTS UNTIL WE ARE FIRST SERVANTS**
   A. High priests worked in bare feet, a sign of servanthood
   B. Hebrews 7:15 - Jesus, doing the dual role of the Priest
   C. He represented men to God, and God to men
   D. You, too, are such a Priest!
   E. Illustration: deacon ministering to a dying man

5. **THE SIGNIFICANCE OF THE PRIEST'S SASH**
   A. Exodus 28:40: worn by all priests
   B. Used by servants to wash feet
      1. John 13:5: used by Jesus for this purpose
      2. Revelation 1:3: Jesus will serve YOU and wash YOUR feet

6. **PRIESTLY SERVANT, GO TO THE WORK!**

DISCUSSION TOPICS

Always begin with your DAILY REPORT TIME
Let each person share briefly;
report insights gained by completing
the Practical Assignment.

WEEKLY REPORT TIME: (10 minutes) Let each person share for no more than 1 minute, reporting insights gained from the Weekly Assignment. Then use the remaining portion of the 10 minutes for a general discussion of your findings.

DISCUSSION QUESTIONS: (30 minutes)

1. Let each person share what this 11 week course has meant in shaping values for living. What new directions are to be travelled as a result?

2. What steps need to be taken to keep from "slipping back" into old patterns, old habits?

3. What should the group do to encourage others in the congregation to take LIFE BASIC TRAINING?

4. This is your last time to meet together. Take some time to share parting blessings with one another.

5. Close with prayer

Jesus then came up and spoke to them. He said: "Full authority in heaven and on earth has been committed to me. Go forth therefore and make all nations my disciples; baptize men everywhere in the name of the Father and the Son and the Holy Spirit, and teach them to observe all that I have commanded you. And be assured, I am with you always, to the end of time."

Matthew 28:18-20

PRACTICAL ASSIGNMENT

Let each take care how he builds. There can be no other foundation beyond that which is already laid; I mean Jesus Christ himself. If anyone builds on that foundation with gold, silver, and fine stone, or with wood, hay, and straw, the work that each man does will at last be brought to light; the day of judgment will expose it. For that day dawns in fire, and the fire will test the worth of each man's work. If a man's building stands, he will be rewarded; if it burns, he will have to bear the loss; and yet he will escape with his life, as one might from a fire. Surely you know that you are God's temple, where the Spirit of God dwells.

I Corinthians 3:10-16

DAILY GROWTH GUIDE

PRIESTLY LIVING

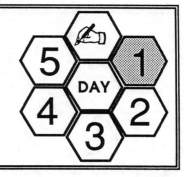

DAY ONE: SERVING AS PRIESTS OF GOD

SCRIPTURE READING: REVELATION 1:5-6

1. **According to these verses, why are we released from our sins?**

2. **Who do we serve as priests? (verse 6)**
   - ☐ Our church
   - ☐ Our God and Father
   - ☐ Our family

3. **Who is to be glorified by our priesthood? (verse 6)**

4. **By definition, a "priest" represents GOD to MAN, MAN to GOD:**

   Name three persons to whom you minister as God's priest:

   1.

   2.

   3.

THOUGHT FOR THE DAY:
NO GREATER MINISTRY EXISTS THAN BEING GOD'S REPRESENTATIVE TO THE SONS OF ADAM! YOU ARE A ROYAL PRIEST...MEANING THAT YOU ARE A CHILD OF THE KING, MAKING YOU ROYALTY...AND YOU ARE A SERVANT, MAKING YOU A PRIEST!

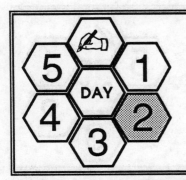

DAILY GROWTH GUIDE

PRIESTLY LIVING

DAY TWO: REPRESENTING MEN BEFORE GOD

SCRIPTURE READING: ROMANS 9:1-3; 10:1

In these passages, Paul's deep, intense desire for Israel's salvation is communicated to us. Reflect upon the intensity of his "priestly heart" before answering the questions below.

1. **Which words describe Paul's concern for Israel?**

   ☐ Disgust with their unbelief

   ☐ Great sorrow over their unbelief

   ☐ Endless frustration with their rejection of Christ

   ☐ Unceasing grief because of their rejection of Christ

2. **As a priest - standing between man and God - what price would Paul pay to bring them to a personal faith in Christ? (9:3)**

3. **In 10:1, we have an example of "Priestly Praying." For what do priests pray?**

4. **In a sentence or two, rephrase these verses to express your own priestly burden for the three persons you listed yesterday:**

> **THOUGHT FOR THE DAY:**
> *"PRIESTLY PRAYING" INVOLVES STANDING BETWEEN SINFUL MEN AND AN HOLY GOD WITH A BROKEN HEART. INTERCESSION FOR OTHERS IS AN OVERWHELMING TASK. BEING IN A PRAYER MEETING WHERE EVERY PERSON IS A PRIEST, AND ALL THE PRAYING IS PRIESTLY INTERCESSION FOR SINFUL MEN, IS AN UNFORGETTABLE EXPERIENCE!*

DAILY GROWTH GUIDE

PRIESTLY LIVING

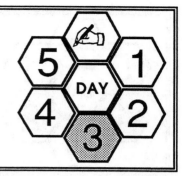

DAY THREE: OUR PRIESTLY SACRIFICE
SCRIPTURE READING: HEBREWS 13:15

1. What sacrifice are we to make as priests?

2. Read the following quotation from Barclay:
"When a man offered a sin-offering he was trying to get something out of God, forgiveness for his sins, while a thank-offering was the unconditional offering of a grateful heart."

What is our "sin-offering?"
☐ Our tithes to the Lord

☐ Christ's death on the cross

☐ The Lenten Season

3. How is PRAISE a thank-offering, not a sin-offering?
☐ We do it to entice God to forgive our sins

☐ It is the unconditional offering of a grateful heart

4. What is the public statement we priests make by PRAISE?
☐ A statement of unashamed loyalty to Christ

☐ A glad confession of our sonship and servanthood

☐ Both of the above

☐ Either of the above

THOUGHT FOR THE DAY:
"THE CHRISTIAN CAN ALWAYS OFFER TO THE WORLD AND TO GOD A LIFE THAT IS NEVER ASHAMED TO SHOW WHOSE IT IS AND WHOM IT SERVES. NEVER TO BE ASHAMED OF THE GOSPEL OF JESUS CHRIST IS ALSO AN OFFERING."
WILLIAM BARCLAY

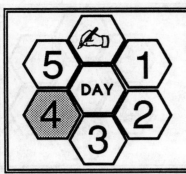

DAILY GROWTH GUIDE

PRIESTLY LIVING

DAY FOUR: MORE ABOUT PRIESTLY SACRIFICE

SCRIPTURE READING: HEBREWS 13:16, 1 THESSALONIANS 2:8

1. What two additional "thank offerings" does the writer list here?

   1.

   2.

**2. "Doing good" - does it sound trite? Substitute "deeds of kindness..."
Think again of the three names you listed in Day One's material.
List three "deeds of kindness" which would be "priestly ministry" to them:**

   1.

   2.

   3.

**3. How does 1Thessalonians 2:8 explain "sharing" or "communication,"
which is the second sacrifice mentioned in our verse?**

**4. What does this verse do to help you understand the importance of priests
developing SHARE GROUPS as a part of their service?**

> *THOUGHT FOR THE DAY:*
> *PARTICIPATING IN A SHARE GROUP IS A PRIESTLY EXPERIENCE. YOUR
> INVOLVEMENT IN "PRIESTLY PRAYING" AND "PRIESTLY SERVICE" WILL
> NOT ONLY BE LIFE-CHANGING FOR SINFUL MEN. IT WILL BE
> LIFE-CHANGING FOR YOU, TOO!*

DAILY GROWTH GUIDE
PRIESTLY LIVING

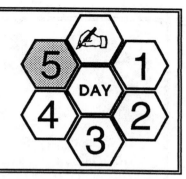

DAY FIVE: ETERNITY? STILL SERVANT-PRIESTS!
SCRIPTURE READING: REVELATION 5:9,10; 20:6

1. According to 5:9, who is included in God's blood-bought family?

2. What will be their title in eternity? (verse 10)

3. According to 20:6, are these priests subject to death?
    ☐ Yes
    ☐ No

4. When does our Priesthood start - at conversion, or in eternity?

5. If you say it started at conversion, how high a priority should you place on your priestly activity TODAY?

THOUGHT FOR THE DAY:
YOU ARE NOW...RIGHT NOW...A PRIEST OF GOD, AND YOU WILL FOREVER BE ONE! MAY YOUR TRAINING FOR THE MINISTRY OF A PRIEST BE A RICH AND LASTING EXPERIENCE.   TOUCH BASIC TRAINING IS THE LAST TRAINING IN EVANGELISM AND MINISTRY YOU WILL EVER NEED TO TAKE. WELCOME, FRIEND, TO THE BEGINNING OF THE REST OF YOUR ETERNAL SERVICE FOR CHRIST!

Thought For The Week

It was early Sunday morning. Warm handshakes and embraces revealed the closeness of these people to each other. For several moments, they shared deep concerns. One person shared about a late night ministry to a near suicide. Another talked about a couple on their street whose marriage was in "white water."

A man told of an evening of fellowship in his home with one of the young attorneys in his law firm, and his extreme skepticism about Christ. They began to fervently engage in prayer together.

Somehow, this was a "different" prayer meeting than all the others I had attended. What made it unique?

THESE WERE "PRIESTLY PRAYERS." For the first time in all the years I had been around Christians, I was praying with a group who were ALL Priests. What made their praying unique?

Why, every single person in the room was interceding for a broken life, and every broken life was attached to a Servant-Priest who had paid the price of ministry with him or her.

I have now experienced dozens of "Priestly Prayer Meetings." That same spine-tingling thrill has recurred in every single one of them. All of them have been distinctively different from the "run of the mill" prayer found in most prayer times.

Your team has been together for 11 weeks. Would you like to continue your journey? Why not become a "Share Group?"

Invite some unbelievers into your team's homes. Spend an evening fellowshipping with them. Learn how to serve them. *Let God begin to use you!*

"Behold, I am coming soon! My reward is with me, and I will give to everyone according to what he has done. I am the Alpha and the Omega, the First and the Last, the Beginning and the End."
● *Revelation 22:12*

A Word About Touch Outreach Ministries

Launched over 20 years ago, Touch Outreach has pioneered in developing Cell Groups for use by those who serve the church as an organism rather than an organization.

When it comes to Cell Groups, no one else has studied, tested, and written more equipping materials that Touch Outreach.

The church that lives as an organism will shape its lifestyle around these three "C's"...

Cells

Composed of no less than 3 and no more than 15 Christians, the Cell functions in the following ways:
- Gathering together weekly to experience worship, prayer, edification and ministry.
- Outreach through lifestyle evangelism and Share Groups—small groups meeting felt-needs of pre-Christians.

Congregation

Composed of 100 to 150 Christians, these are the gathering of Cells for Bible study and growth.

Celebration

This is an event that can occur with a group of cells, congregations, or even a number of Cell Group churches assembling together to worship the Lord and King as the Body of Christ.

The Theological Basis for Cell Groups

The Gospel offers infinitely more than heaven when we die! In its purest form, the "Good News" declares that God is calling out a special people for His name...a people who live in a special relationship with each other. The first act of the newly formed church was to go from house to house, breaking bread, praying, and living in a special way with one another. They knew each other so intimately that they shared possessions, bore one another's burdens, and gave witness to a cynical world that love for God creates a very special love between persons.

Organized church life today tends to stifle this relational witness. The church campus is the only place people see each other.

Intimacy and closeness are lost in endless nonrelational large meetings. Even Sunday School often stifles relationships in our desire to amass more and more Bible knowledge. The witness of the early church was stated by Pliny, who said, "See how they love one another? There is nothing they will not do for each other!"

The Church must become a relational community. Cell groups are the Biblical means to accomplish this! People never know each other fully when meeting in a neutral place. Going from house to house, true relationships are created. But...cell groups can meet in homes and still fail to create intimate, loving connections between God's people.

We can't get away from our cognitive curse! We have become so used to having an agenda when we meet that church groups often boldly move into home cell groups, only to smother the relational life with more Bible study, more listening to tapes, etc. It almost seems we are afraid to assemble without an agenda!

The Bride of Christ needs time to reproduce the Upper Room experience, when 120 gathered for 10 days and ended up becoming one! Their unity witnessed so powerfully to the watching unbelievers that 3,000 were added to their number.

God is a God of relationships. He walked with Adam and Eve in the Garden. He related directly to Abraham and Moses. He personally came in Christ to create a relationship with men. He formed a cell group of 12, and lived His life in its community. From its start, He formed His new body, the Church, into cell groups.

TOUCH OUTREACH MINISTRIES *Catalogue*

CELL CHURCH BOOKS

SKU#	ITEM	LIST PRICE
CGC-B	CELL CHURCH BOOK BUNDLE (Items 1-4 found below) No Quantity Breaks Available	$29.95
CGC-1	WHERE DO WE GO FROM HERE? -A Guidebook for the Cell Group Church	14.95
CGC-2	SHEPHERD'S GUIDEBOOK -Cell Leader's Training Manual	9.95
CGC-3	KNOCKING ON DOORS, OPENING HEARTS -Cell member's training tool for relationship/"oikos" evangelism.	9.95
CGC-4	JOURNEY GUIDE -This pamphlet charts a Cell member's walk with Christ, and allows the Shepherd to evaluate where his cell members are in their spiritual journey and how he can best minister to them.	1.45
CGC-5	SPIRITUAL GIFTS INVENTORY Book & Tape -Charts strengths in gifts through a questionnaire format.	7.95
CGC-6	SPIRITUAL GIFTS INVENTORY (Book Only)	2.39
CGC-7	WELCOME TO YOUR CHANGED LIFE (booklet & scripture packet) Introduces the new believer to life with Christ and the cell.	2.00
CGC-8	JOURNEY INTO DISCIPLESHIP -13 group study sessions on developing target groups through lifestyle evangelism.	3.25
CGC-10	THE WAY HOME -Developed with the help of the International Bible Society. This paperback includes the NIV New Testament with a special 13-unit investigative Bible Study for the seeker.	1.25
CGC-11	"OPENING HEARTS" TRILOGY OF BOOKS -Three "user friendly" books equip three person evangelism "Share Groups" to reach unbelievers with no interest in Christ or the church. By working through this three book series, the Share Group Team reaches beyond limited "OIKOSES" to minister to a hurting world. Purchase by the set—save $1.25 (See below for separate pricing)	11.50
CGC-12	BUILDING BRIDGES, OPENING HEARTS -Forming relationships with unbelievers	4.25
CGC-13	BUILDING GROUPS, OPENING HEARTS -Forming groups with unbelievers contacted during "bridge building".	4.25
CGC-14	BUILDING AWARENESS, OPENING HEARTS (Release Date July, 1992) -Penetrating the"oikos" of group members.	4.25
CGC-15	NEW! JESUS SAYS "FOLLOW ME" Introduces children to a new relationship with Christ and the cell group.	2.00

QUANTITY DISCOUNTS ON BOOKS!

We Provide the following discounts for quantity purchases of a single title	10-20 = 10%Off	21-30 = 20% Off	31 or more = 30% Off

CALL FOR BOOKSTORE DISCOUNTS (Bookstore Tax or EIN Number Required)

CELL CHURCH CASSETTES

SKU#	ITEM	LIST PRICE
CGC-16	DION ROBERT ON CELL GROUP CHURCHES -Three interviews Dr. Neighbour conducted with Dion Robert, pastor of one of the largest Cell Churches in Africa, located in Abidjan, Ivory Coast. Translated from French to English (3-60 Minute Tapes)	15.00
CGC-17	THE CELL GROUP STRATEGY -This series is constantly revised as Dr. Neighbour conducts live Seminars. It explains the theology and methodology of the Cell Group Church as it exists today. This includes paper masters of transparencies used in the presentations. Pastors or leadership teams may use this to grasp the concept of Cell life or to explain it to church members. Especially helpful for your members who aren't readers! (5-60 Minute Tapes & Transparency Masters)	25.00
CGC-18	NEW WINESKINS FOR FUTURE CHURCHES -Teachings on Cell Group Church principles at Columbia Biblical Seminary by Dr. Neighbour. Excellent introduction to cell concepts. (2-60 Minute Tapes)	10.00

MC/VISA AND C.O.D. CUSTOMERS-
CALL IN YOUR ORDER TOLL FREE 1-800-735-5865
QUESTIONS? CALL OUR LOCAL LINE (713) 497-7901

T O U C H   M A T E R I A L S

HOW DO TOUCH MATERIALS FIT INTO MY CELL CHURCH PLAN?

Touch Materials were originally designed to introduce a program-based church to share groups. Since then, new materials have been developed which are found on page one. Many pastors use the Touch Materials along with the new materials as special training courses for leadership and staff members. Recently a pastor shared with us that Life Basic Training was very effective in helping his leadership team evaluate their value systems and their vision for the cell church. Another pastor is using the Touch Ministries Seminar to introduce cell life at Spiritual Formation Weekends before interested folks join a cell group. We recommend that you personally evaluate the Touch Materials before investing in the facilitators' kits. The Touch Student Package was specifically designed for this purpose.

TOUCH MINISTRIES SEMINAR (TMS) is a weekend-long seminar designed to help members of a PBD (Program-Based Design) church understand Life Basic Training and Touch Basic Training.

LIFE BASIC TRAINING (LBT) helps Christians re-examine their values from a Biblical perspective. LBT can be used with either the video or audio segments, in a church setting or in small groups.

TOUCH BASIC TRAINING (TBT) is for mature Christians ready to minister to unbelievers who are "turned off" by Christians and the Church. This 20-week training will guide "Share Group" teams to form a 10-week gathering for reaching people the church now leaves untouched.

SKU#	ITEM	LIST PRICE
T-1	TOUCH STUDENT SAMPLE PACKAGE	$49.95
	-Includes all student material for the TOUCH MINISTRIES SEMINAR, LIFE BASIC TRAINING & TOUCH BASIC TRAINING. In addition, Dr. Neighbour has prepared 12 hours of audio cassette tapes that guide the student through TMS and TBT. The package also includes a video sampler that will show the importance of the video segments in the material.	
T-2	TMS FACILITATOR'S KIT	37.50
	-Includes 3 audiotapes, 1 videotape, printed instructions, transparency masters	
T-3	LBT FACILITATOR'S KIT	149.95
	-Includes 6 audiotapes, 2 videotapes, printed instructions, transparency masters	
T-4	TBT FACILITATOR'S KIT	249.95
	-Includes 12 audiotapes, 3 videotapes, printed instructions, transparency masters	
T-5	TMS STUDENT LOOSELEAF WORKBOOKS	4.50
T-6	LBT STUDENT PAPERBACK WORKBOOKS	7.95
T-7	TBT STUDENT KIT	19.95
	-Includes looseleaf text and tracts, pin & doorplate bearing the Touch logo.	

T O U C H   S P E C I A L T Y   I T E M S

SKU#	ITEM	LIST PRICE
M-1	TOUCH LOGO TIE TAC OR LADIES PENDANT	$2.95
	-Write in your choice on order form	
M-2	TOUCH LOGO PLEXIGLASS DOOR PLATES	2.95
M-3	TOUCH LOGO STICKERS (3-COLOR)	.50
M-4	TRACTS (30 OF A SINGLE TITLE)	1.95
	-Write in your choice on order form–available in Spanish & English "Master Plan" "Seed Sowing"(English Only) "Perfect Circle"	
M-5	"I AM CRUCIFIED WITH CHRIST" (2 AUDIOTAPES) -Includes pocket sized illustrated booklet.	9.95
M-6	"IS IT FAIR?" (2 AUDIOTAPES) -Why are the heathen condemned?	9.95
M-7	GODS OF POWER -by Dr. Phil Steyne	14.95
	Most comprehensive work on animism ever written!	
M-8	BRISBANE URBAN STRATEGY REPORT	24.95
M-9	AUCKLAND URBAN STRATEGY REPORT	24.95
M-10	TOUCH OUTREACH VIDEO SAMPLER	FREE
	We have created a videotape that shows segments of our video materials and explains why our ministry has come into existence. $25 deposit on your Visa/MC, fully refunded if returned within 6 weeks of receipt.	

In traditional church life, the only people who are exposed to a Bible Survey course are those who go away to college, Bible school, or seminary. In contrast, a Cell Group Church seeks to equip every member for personal Bible study and research.

After 17 years of testing and revisions, TOUCH OUTREACH MINISTRIES has produced a 488 page, 52-week guidebook to do this effectively. Each week, 9 to 10 pages are covered. This is done in daily study, as the Cell members listen to a 5-minute a day audiotape presentation of the materials.

We recommend that Cell Church pastors order our scripts and tape them for distribution to all Cell members. TOUCH OUTREACH MINISTRIES will assist you in tape duplication, or you may make copies on your own. Two weeks of study will fit on one 60-minute cassette. These tapes are then checked out one at a time through your church library or book table. A complete set for everyone in your cell church is not necessary–just stagger the program by two weeks and make a small quantity of duplicates. To receive the next two week study, the member will simply exchange tapes, and a new member can begin. Cover the Bible has been used successfully both in a classroom setting and as a part of the "Equipping Time" which precedes the Cell Group meeting.

For bulk orders of books, significant discounts are offered. Purchase of the scripts for one-time use is done through a licensing arrangement.

C O V E R   T H E   B I B L E

SKU#	ITEM	LIST PRICE
CTB-1	COVER THE BIBLE NOTEBOOKS (Looseleaf)	$19.95
	Use this version if you're going to hand out units by the week	
CTB-2	COVER THE BIBLE PAPERBACK	$15.95
CTB-3	56-HOUR CASSETTE LECTURES	$169.95
CTB-4	52-WEEK CASSETTE BROADCASTS	$169.95
CTB-5	COVER THE BIBLE VOICE SCRIPTS	$100.00
	Record you own COVER THE BIBLE teaching tapes, to be heard 5 minutes daily, 5 days a week for a year. You'll create 26 tapes, 2 weeks per tape. Let your cell members be taught personally by you! (Not for use on radio)	
CTB-6	NIV STUDY BIBLE, Hardback ($34.95 retail)	$28.00
CTB-7	Amazing STUDENT MAP MANUAL ($39.95 retail)	$19.95

O R D E R   B L A N K

SKU #	QUANTITY & DESCRIPTION	UNIT COST	TOTAL COST

PLEASE SHIP MY ORDER:
- ☐ UPS GROUND
- ☐ UPS GROUND C.O.D. (Add $3.75)
- ☐ U.S. POST OFFICE DOMESTIC
- ☐ U.S. POST OFFICE FOREIGN Surface Mail
- ☐ U.S. POST OFFICE FOREIGN Air Mail

INTERNATIONAL ORDERS USE VISA/MC OR U.S. CHECKING ACCOUNT

SUBTOTAL	
SHIPPING/ HANDLING	
C.O.D. CHARGES (IF ANY)	
TOTAL	

U.S. POST OFFICE SHIPPING

U.S. & TERRITORIES
Up to $20 = $2.00
$21-50 = $4.00
Over $50 = 8% of total

2-3 WEEK DELIVERY-BOOK RATE

CANADA
Up to $35 = $5.00
Over $35 = 15% of total

OVERSEAS - SEA MAIL
(2-5 Month Delivery)
Up to $25 = $5.00
Over $25 = 25% of total

OVERSEAS - AIR MAIL
100% OF TOTAL

PLEASE READ THIS BEFORE ORDERING ...

Payment policy: We require prepayment on all orders by check or VISA/MC. We are unable to invoice you or a church. Sorry!

Price Guarantee: Prices in this Catalogue are guaranteed through 12/31/92. Most prices don't change; we'll adjust any that do. The prices found in this catalogue replace all pricing from previous catalogues or price lists. We are not responsible for typographical errors.

Backorders: As much as we try, it's not always possible to keep all titles in stock. If we cannot ship within 60 days, we will refund your money.

Returns: At our low prices, **we cannot permit returns**. However, if your materials are damaged in shipping, defective, or incorrectly shipped, we will gladly replace them.

UPS SHIPPING

AL, AR, CO, FL, IA, KS, LA, MN, MS, MO, ND, NE, OK, SD, TX, WY,
Up to $20 = $2.00
$21-50 = $4.00
Over $50 = 8% of total

DE, DC, GA, IL, IN, KY, MD, MI, NC, OH, SC, TN, VA, WI, WV
Up to $20 = $2.50
$21-50 = $5.00
Over $50 = 11% of total

AZ, CA, ID, MT, NM, NV, OR, UT, WA
Up to $20 = $3.00
$21-50 = $6.00
Over $50 = 14% of total

CT, MA, ME, NH, NJ, NY, PA, RI, VT
Up to $20 = $3.50
$21-50 = $7.00
Over $50 = 18% of total

CALL FOR NEXT DAY & 2 DAY AIR RATES

**MAIL TO: TOUCH OUTREACH MINISTRIES
P.O. BOX 19888 ■ HOUSTON, TX 77224
(713) 497-7901**

YOUR ACCT/REF. # _____

NAME _____

CHURCH _____

STREET ADDRESS (P.O. BOXES ONLY IF WE ARE TO SHIP THROUGH THE U.S. POST OFFICE)

_____

CITY _____ STATE _____ ZIP _____

BUSINESS PHONE: (_____) _____

HOME PHONE: (_____) _____

CHECK NUMBER _____

CHARGE MY: ☐ VISA   ☐ MASTERCARD

MY NUMBER ☐☐☐☐ ☐☐☐☐ ☐☐☐☐ ☐☐☐☐

EXPIRATION DATE _____ / _____

PRINT YOUR NAME BELOW EXACTLY AS IT APPEARS CARD

_____

YOUR SIGNATURE _____